Letters From An American Woman

Nancy L. Carter & CJ Elam

Research by Deanna Campbell

Introduction:

Hello My Fellow Americans,

If your curiosity has gotten the best of you, then you are probably standing in the middle of an isle in your local bookstore thumbing through this book wondering what may lie in wait for you within these pages. Let me give you a heads up. My best friend and I wrote this book in the hope of opening the eyes of at least a few of you. Not just to what our government is attempting to do, (and sometimes succeeding) behind our backs, but also to some of the day to day issues most American families face. Every where she and I go, we people watch. We make observations to behaviors and wonder why people behave the way they do. We often wonder how our grandparents would react to some of these situations. Admit it, you've done this. You wouldn't still be holding this book if you hadn't. If you are still reading, allow me to give you fair warning. Some of the material in these pages may get your dander up; it may make you fighting mad or absolutely infuriate you. If it does; good! That is the point.

Our philosophy is if a situation gets under your skin then maybe you will take an activist approach in attempt to change that situation. Thomas Jefferson said "Every generation needs a new revolution." We are firm believers in this. No, we aren't highly educated, and we come from humble, meager backgrounds. We have both suffered the ill effects of a government education, and we have both worked our way up to where we are now from nothing. In fact, we are still in the process of this, hence the book you are now staring at dumbfounded and wondering "Are these people for real?" Yes, we are for real and if you keep reading you will understand.

So, take your new found treasure to the check out, go home, turn the ringer and TV off, and get comfortable. You are in for a wild and eye opening ride. This ride we speak of will educate you on some of the backdoor deals our elected politicians are trying to implement "for our own good", the degeneration of today's society, the mistreatment of our American heroes, and many other topics. You will laugh. You will scream. You will wonder "How is this possible?" You might get scared. You may even shed a tear or two. There is some material in the confines of this book that may even offend.   This is not intentional, of course. However, if you do find yourself offended, you may want to consider why. Besides which, in this great nation we like to call the United States of America you have every right to be offended and we have every right to freedom of speech.

Everything in this book is written for three reasons. 1) Our faith in GOD. 2) Our kids. 3) Our patriotism. These are the driving forces behind everything we do. Enjoy.

Chapter 1

Letters to America

The America We Miss.

"Even peace may be purchased at too high a price."

Benjamin Franklin

Dear Fellow Americans:

My name is Nancy Carter, and until recently, I was a sheep. Yes, I said it. I used to be a victim of our government's WMDs (Weapons of Mass Distraction). I mean music, movies, TV, sports, magazines, and my personal favorite, books. All of these things and so many more serve one purpose, and one purpose only: To distract American Citizens from what is really happening. Don't know what I'm talking about? Look around you; watch Fox News once in a while. You'll see what I mean.

Today is the Fourth of July, and as I watched the fireworks displays around my house, and listened to the laughter and squeals of delight from the neighborhood children, I am struck by what truly is a terrifying thought. It occurs to me how complacent we as American citizens have become. The Fourth of July is not just a day to cook out, party, and set off fireworks. It is the day that our forefathers declared our independence. It was the day that they stood up as one, and said, "Enough!" to tyranny. Now, today, it's become just another commercialized holiday. We all need to get back to the basics. We need to remember that men bled and died because they believed that "All men are created equal, and endowed *by our Creator* with certain inalienable rights...life, liberty, and the pursuit of happiness." We lost sight of that somewhere along the way. When I think of whom we once were as a nation, and compare that to who we are now, it breaks my heart. I love this country, and all that for which it stands, but sometimes I wonder if I am part of a very small minority...

When Barack Obama first announced that he would be running for president, I was a little excited, I mean, how could I not be, right? Then I started paying attention to the things that he said and did. I watched his celebrity grow by leaps and bounds. The whole "Obamessiah" thing scared me, though. The fact that people actually saw him as a savior. He's a human being, nothing more. So while millions of people were being swept up in an almost religious fervor for this guy, I was turned off. He seemed so disingenuous, and there were a lot of things about him that I found discomfiting. I tried to do research on him, you know, to find out what he was really all about, but to no avail. I couldn't find anything on him that wasn't common knowledge. That didn't seem right either. I mean, you can always dig up dirt on the internet, right? But what could I do? I spoke out against him to anyone who would listen, and, of course, I voted for the woman (Palin). Other than that, I could only sit back and watch as events played out on the political stage.

During the course of all of this, my unease grew steadily. I didn't know quite what the problem was, but I knew it was something big. Even if I couldn't find anything else on the man, what we did know was too much for me. They say that you can judge a man by the company that he keeps, and Wright, Rezco, and Ayers were the people with whom Obama spent large portions of his time. Need I say more? Still, there were those who said "Give him a chance", and "You don't know him". So, I continued to watch and wait.

I didn't have to wait very long. Immediately upon taking office, he began to utterly destroy our nation's economy.

His "Stimulus Plan" was enough to ensure that our economy will not recover for several generations. He has crippled the private sector, and weakened our government nearly beyond repair. At first I thought to myself, "Can he really be this ignorant? This is lunacy. Surely someone will correct him!" I thought it was all a product of his inexperience, and naiveté, but I was wrong. As time went on, I could see that Obama's actions are not folly at all. He knows exactly what he is doing.

Since its inception, the United Nations has been trying to get the U. S. under its aegis, or control, but our government, and more importantly, our citizens have resisted. We refused to give up our sovereignty. So what better way to force us into submission than to destroy us from the inside out? Destroy us economically, and weaken our military, and we will have no choice but to ask the UN for help.

People become upset over what has been termed a redistribution of wealth, but what we fail to see is that it is actually a redistribution of power. America has, traditionally, been a world superpower, and as such, a major thorn in the side of the Globalization movement. The American Spirit has been the single largest obstacle to the achievement of a global government. Remove our might, and the Globalists can finally achieve their goals.

And that's where the WMDs come in. They distract us so that we don't notice what's going on behind the scenes. "Pay no attention to the man behind the curtain...." The American people have been deceived for decades. What we don't see is that since WWII we have been moving closer and closer to what George HW Bush termed "A New World Order". And under George W Bush, we took our biggest steps yet. With the inception of the Department Homeland Security, the Patriot Act, and the North American Union, Bush singlehandedly stripped the citizens of this country of more rights and freedoms than any other before him. Before now, he was the biggest threat to our nation's sovereignty, and our individual rights as citizens. Under the Patriot Act, the president has the Authority to enact martial law at any time, for any reason that he deems to be an "emergency". In other words, the swine flu would have been sufficient cause. Under that same act, breaking *any* law, local, state or federal, can be construed as an act of terrorism. That's right, even something as minor as jaywalking, or speeding. Don't believe me? Read it for yourself. You'd be amazed. I know I was.

Now we have our "savior', the "Anointed One", Barack Obama. The 700 Billion dollar stimulus package, Cap and Trade, Obamacare, and now they are talking about the possibility of a *second* stimulus plan. Honestly, we can't afford this much "help". But he knows that. As I said before, it's all by design. Additionally, there is a rumor floating around that some of his followers are trying to find a way to circumvent the 22nd Amendment. If you don't know what that Amendment is, it's the one that limits a president to *two-* four year terms, or eight total years in office. So instead of President Obama, he would be Dictator Obama, or King Obama. I don't know how much, if any, truth there is to that rumor. We shall see.

What's next on the agenda? I don't know, but I can guarantee that it won't be anything that's actually good for America.

So if you're still wondering who I am, I am first and foremost, a child of God, second, a citizen of The United States of America, third, a staunch Constitutionalist, and fourth, AWARE.

Don't be like I was. I actually believed that our government was looking out for the best interests of its citizens. I believed that, even if I didn't agree with what they were doing, they had access to information that I didn't have, and so must be making the best decisions that they could. At least, that's what I told myself. The truth is I was just too intimidated to get involved. I was just one person. What could I say or do that would make a bit of difference?

I realize now that one voice, lifted up and refusing to be silenced can stir other voices to join, and soon, you will have a choir, all singing in harmony. When you have that, people have no choice but to either listen up, or drown you out. Either way, you've got their attention.

Add your voice the choir that says "We will not stand idly by, while our country is thrown to the ravenous wolves."

Patriotically yours,

NLC

Dear America:

I am writing to you with the hope of opening the eyes of at least a few. I have a heavy heart at the moment. Every time I turn on the television or the radio or open a newspaper, it only gets worse. I, like so many of you, grew up thinking this is the greatest country on Earth. Well, it is. The problem was that, again like you, I was deluded into thinking that the greatness of this country was secure. It's not.

The utopian fantasy of security and a caring government was soon shattered after I got out on my own and had a little one depending on me. It was then that I started paying attention to what was going on in the world around. Yes, sad to say, I was a sheep caught in the snare of WMD's. In other words, I dumbly did as I was told like a lamb being led to the slaughter, and was only interested in the weapons of mass distraction. When I actually woke up and started using the mass of grey goo that God placed in my thick skull, I felt as if I had been hit by a Mack truck. Yeah, that's right. There I was standing in my living room with a toddler attached to my leg thinking, "Did anyone get the license plate number?" I soon realized the number was 1600 Pennsylvania. For those of you who may not know this bit of trivia, that is the White House.

I was overwhelmed by the flood of realization. I felt a lot like what an over stimulated nine month must feel like. Then came the intense need to do something about it. So like a good patriotic citizen, I registered to vote. I soon participated in my first presidential election. I was so proud that I had voted for the right person. However, before long I could hear a little voice in the back of my mind asking "Is there really a right person?" Who are these people the media parades in front of us and where do they come from? I know that not just anyone can wake up one day and decide to run for president. I know that these people are supposed to be completely vetted before they can make a serious bid for that office. The problem is that the vetting process is becoming more and more one sided.

In addition to that, during the aftermath of Hurricane Katrina, I finally realized that the root of the problem is far deeper than the office of president. People everywhere were trying to assign blame, and the person who seemed the scapegoat was the president. I kept thinking to myself, "This man isn't God; he can't control the weather." The fact is, the tragedy of Hurricane Katrina could not be blamed on one person, or even one government agency. It was a massive communication and infrastructure breakdown that turned a bad situation into a tragedy that affected millions. All the while, people were asking why the evacuations weren't successful, why warnings weren't issued sooner, and how were the levies breached. The governor waited to ask for federal assistance. The mayor didn't utilize all assets at his disposal to evacuate people. Also discussed at great length was the issue of levy maintenance. But in the end, it all pointed back to the president.

I remember, ages ago, learning about checks and balances in school. There are three parts to our government; the executive, the legislative and the judicial branches. The president is only part of one of these branches. He is like a failsafe. The Senate and House of Representatives are responsible for writing and passing the bills or House Resolutions that later become laws. That's where our questions need to be directed. Do you even know who your state senators and congressmen are? I didn't. I ashamed to say I was an uneducated voter. I had no idea who these people were let alone what they stood for, or what they were doing for my state. Someone once said knowledge is power. This is true. So I educated myself.

In the process of educating myself, I came to the realization that these people are my employees. Have you ever thought about it that way? You should. We all should. We, as citizens, vote them into office. It is their job to do what is in the best interests of the country. We pay the taxes that pay their salaries. According to the Constitution, they answer to us. We also have the right to remove them from these offices if they don't do what they were elected to do. If you think I'm joking, read the Constitution for yourself. After all, if your education was anything like mine, the farthest you've gotten into that document was the Preamble or, if you were blessed enough to have a good teacher, maybe part of the Bill of Rights. That leads into another major question. Do you know what is in the first ten amendments? You should. These are the fundamental rights that our founding fathers put into place; the very rights that our current government has been trying to strip away from us.

Here is what I propose: All schools should be mandated to teach these documents in their entirety. I also think you should be required to know the fundamentals of how this government is supposed to work before you are allowed to get your voter card. First and foremost though, we need to get back to basics. We need to go back to what the forefathers intended for this country. If it takes a grassroots movement to do it; so be it. Fellow Americans, we need to wake up. You may think like I once did "I am only one person, what can I possibly do?" I am here to tell you: you can do a lot. If every single person were to take their role as a citizen seriously and get involved, this country would be far greater than it is today.

Call your representatives. Write them; email them, do whatever it takes. Let them know how you feel and what you want. Follow up and make sure they perform to your expectations. If they don't, fire them. Find a way to remove them from office. Every one vote has the power of many. I would say this is a call to arms but someone might take me literally. And, well, we do not need violence. We were given the tools to make these changes peacefully in the documents that our founding fathers laid as a foundation for this great nation. Once these actions have been put into place, teach your children. Don't leave it to the government to do so. That is what they want. The uneducated are easily manipulated and controllable. Don't be like I was. Stand up and fight for the right to control your own path. In doing so, you will allow your children the benefit of enjoying the freedoms we enjoyed as children. What better gift could you possibly give?

With that thought I will leave you for now, but rest assured, I am watching and listening. I am doing both my patriotic duty and my duty as a parent. I implore you to do the same.

Patriotically yours,

C.J. Elam

Chapter 2

The Real American Heroes

A Tribute to Our Military

"There is a certain enthusiasm in liberty that makes human nature rise above itself, in acts of bravery and heroism."

Alexander Hamilton

Duty and Honor

Those two words are two of the most powerful words in the English language. But what do they mean? For some, they are just words, for others, they are tools to manipulate people into action, and for still others, they describe a way of life. There are those who wake up every morning, in a country that is not their own, fighting for a cause that is not their own, because of those two words.

We both come from military families, and while neither of us has ever served in our armed forces, we each have family members who are. We both know what it's like to watch a loved one board a bus that will take them to a plane that will take them thousands of miles from home, and into a war zone. We know what it's like to become instantly nauseated and afraid if the phone rings in the middle of the night. Or, in some cases, if it doesn't. We've seen what war does to our loved ones, and known the heartache of not being able to help. More importantly, we know we are not the only ones.

What bothers us is the fact that, if a celebrity overdoses on drugs, its news. If some brave soldier is killed while trying to protect someone else's freedom, we don't even hear his/her name. We ask you, what do celebrities do that is so great? Why should they be held in higher esteem than those who lay their lives on the line daily to fight for this country, and the cause of freedom around the world? We are convinced that, if the news media of this country would give half as much attention to them as is given to celebrities, more people would understand what duty and honor truly mean. They are not just abstract ideas, or pretty words used to make politicians sound patriotic. They have real, personal, powerful meaning behind them, and it's time that we as Americans open our eyes and see that.

Webster's defines duty as: (1) respect or obedience to be shown to one's parents, elders, etc. (2) any act required by one's position, or by moral or legal considerations, etc. (3) service, especially military /overseas duty

Honor is defined as follows: (1) high regard or respect, especially (a) glory; fame (b) good reputation (2) integrity (3) chastity (4) high rank; distinction (5) a source of respect or fame.

We say that it is our duty as American citizens to honor the men and women of our armed forces, not only in word, but also in deed. Each of us should take the time to do something for a friend, neighbor, or relative who has witnessed and taken a stand against horrors that you and I can only imagine. Thanking them is not enough. Those words are empty. We should make sure that they know how much their sacrifice means to us. Support them as they return from war torn nations, and try to reintegrate themselves into our society. We owe it to each and every one of them.

The Soldier's Conflict

Have you ever stopped to wonder why it is that our service men and women have such a hard time reintegrating into society after serving in a war? For the longest time, I didn't know, I mean, not really. Sure, in some abstract way I knew that it had to be tough to adjust from war to peace. Sadly, I just never really thought about it. Or if I did, I somewhat cold heartedly thought that they got exactly what they signed up for. I could not have been more wrong. For all the veterans reading this, I apologize from the bottom of my heart. Thanks to a conversation with my sister in-law, I have opened my eyes.

It all started with the possibility of her dad serving yet another tour overseas. He's already served three. She is understandably upset, and afraid that her dad is looking for the battle that he can't win. You know, go out in a blaze of glory, so to speak. In the process of trying to soothe her fears, I came to a startling revelation.

We as a country do the unthinkable every day. We first make killers, then punish them. Yeah, I know. It's sophomoric. But think about it. We train men to go into the worst conditions and commit heinous acts, all in the name of our country. We then expect these men to come home and go about their normal lives as if those things never happened. If these men were to do those same things within the normal bounds of society, they would be punished, swiftly and surely. It's only okay if they have a government sanction.

The problem is this: how does a man stop being what he's been for twenty years? How can he forget that he used to be a professional killer? The answer is, he can't.

We need to see that. These men put their lives in jeopardy and do things that most of us can't even imagine, just to keep us safe. They give up their innocence, and any chance at normalcy to defend our freedoms. Many of them leave behind families, and risk turning their wives to widows and their children to orphans, because they believe in this country.

Do you have any idea of the scope of that sacrifice? Do you know what kind of lasting effect that has on a person? Can you honestly say that you understand what they are going through, if you have never been there? No, you can't. You have no idea. You sit in your nice, air conditioned house, watch the news on your big screen television, and don't even bat an eye when the anchor tells you that we have lost over 4000 service men and women to a war we can't win. We have no concept of what it's like to watch our friends get shot, stabbed, or blown apart. We will never understand the effects of having to kill men, women, and sometimes children, just to stay alive. Oh sure, we say "thank a vet for his or her service." Yes, we should thank them, but we should also realize that our thanks will never be enough. These people don't want our platitudes. The best way that we can show them our appreciation is by not squandering what they sacrifice so much to protect. Get on your knees and thank God that, for the moment, you live in "the land of the free, and the home of the brave." Thank Him for the men and women who give their lives in defense of what we take for granted. Then, do whatever you can to make life easier for them. They deserve that, and so very much more.

NLC

With special thanks to the vets in my life: Donny Covey, Steven Davis, Adam Fields, Quenten Kester, Edward E. Robinson, and many others.

Disposable Heroes

I recently heard a senator on TV say that the military has the best healthcare in the country. Well, I beg to differ. There are very few good things about this system. It covers a lot (barely), but the paperwork and red tape involved is ridiculous. Not to mention the headaches that are a natural part of dealing with the government. Allow me to explain.

Did you know that the company who handles Tricare is Humana Health? You may ask why that's so important. Here's why. Humana Health is the insurance provider that is responsible for Medicare and Medicaid. This, in turn, means two things:

1. Care is provided with the same "efficiency" as Medicaid and Medicare. (And we all know how bad those systems are.)
2. If a person covered under Tricare chooses to see a civilian doctor, the doctor is only paid a small percentage of what they would be paid by private sector insurance.

Here is an example. I know a soldier who was recently injured during a training exercise while serving overseas. He was evaluated by the on post medical personnel only to have them postpone the treatment that he needed. Several months later, he was sent back stateside to proceed with medical treatment. The *Military hospital* that he was sent to was substandard at best. While he was a patient of this facility, a young PFC had a back surgery which left him completely immobile. The day following his surgery, he was moved out of the hospital and into the barracks, ostensibly to empty the bed for other wounded soldiers. However, due to this move, the young man had no continued care. Had it not been for the other soldiers housed in his barracks, this man who was injured in the line of duty would not have been able to eat, bathe, or even change clothes. He would have been lying in his own waste. None of the medical staff brought him meals, or even bothered to check on him. Fortunately, the other soldiers were compassionate, and the young PFC did not have to suffer the effects of this facility's incompetence.

After witnessing this affront to all servicemen and women, my friend demanded to be sent home for his medical care. (As a National Guard member, he has the right to do that.) It was then left up to his wife to contact the CBHCO (Community Based Health Care Organization) program, due to the fact that the facility he was in refused to do so on his behalf. After a month of red tape, he and his wife were finally able to get him transferred home to his local Guard Unit. They then proceeded with his medical care through the private sector, under the supervision of the military. Unfortunately, using the private sector did not guarantee them the right to make any choices, such as:

1. The surgeon
2. The hospital
3. The Treatments
4. Or the any of the follow up treatments.

The military refused him the right to choose his surgeon, because there happened to be another surgeon who had a patient opening two days earlier than the surgeon he wanted to use. Needless to say, the surgeon the military chose was completely inept. (Not to mention the fact that during the first appointment, this doctor made a very rude, degrading remark about the National Guard. "Are you in the real Army or the fake Army?" Rumor has it that this particular doctor was only able to get his medical license because of the fact that the minimum standards for military personnel to be accepted into Medical Graduate School are significantly lower than private students.) Throughout the course of his treatment, they kept receiving letters from Tricare stating that they had changed his Primary Care Physician, and because he didn't have a referral from his new PCP, they would not pay for his treatment. This happened on three separate occasions. Each time, he and his wife had to call Tricare and explain the situation to them all over again. It makes me wonder how many other soldiers have had to go through this.

Now, after three different surgeries and three different surgeons, he is still unable to perform the duties of his civilian job. In fact, during a town hall meeting with the soldiers in the CBHCO program, he and several others who still needed medical care were told that if they could walk, they were being cut loose. What is that? As a result of this, he was released and returned to work against his *physician's* advice. What's worse is the fact that this story is only one of thousands. There are many others. If you don't believe me, ask any disabled veteran.

How is it that we allow the men and women who serve and protect this nation to bear this ongoing insult? Why have the men and women in Washington not done anything to "reform" this system? They talk a lot about how much they appreciate our soldiers, but then they make those same soldiers deal with ineptitude and incompetence as repayment for the sacrifices that they have made. It is abominable.

CJE

Chapter 3

The Founding Documents

The Declaration of Independence, The Constitution of the United States, and The Bill of Rights.

Founding Documents

You may be wondering why we have chosen to devote an entire chapter to the nation's founding documents. For too long, the citizenry of this country has neglected the history of this great nation. How can we expect to preserve the cornerstone of our government and freedoms, if we don't know what that cornerstone is? Therefore, we feel that it is important to include a reminder nation's humble beginnings.

In this chapter, we will examine these documents, one by one, break them down, and interpret each one, line by line. Because we believe that these documents cannot be properly interpreted or fully understood without the proper context, we will include quotes from the founding fathers wherever possible.

We hope that you find this chapter enlightening, and not too dry. We also hope that you will find in this section, a love and a passion for this country that you didn't know you had. We did. Writing this chapter has made us even more determined to do whatever possible to preserve the greatest nation on Earth: The United States of America.

Declaration of Independence

The unanimous Declaration of the thirteen united States of America,

When in the Course of human events, it becomes necessary for one people to dissolve the political bands which have connected them with another, and to assume among the powers of the earth, the separate and equal station to which the Laws of Nature and of Nature's God entitle them, a decent respect to the opinions of mankind requires that they should declare the causes which impel them to the separation.

This first section is pretty self explanatory. It says that, should the need arise for one nation (state, people) to separate itself from another and assume sovereignty; dignity dictates that those reasons should be declared openly.

We hold these truths to be self-evident, that all men are created equal, that they are endowed by their Creator with certain unalienable Rights, that among these are Life, Liberty and the pursuit of Happiness

We, as human beings, are God's creation, and as such, are created equal, and with certain rights that no one can take away from us. Examples of these rights include, but are not limited to: Life, liberty, and the pursuit of happiness.

That to secure these rights, Governments are instituted among Men, deriving their just powers from the consent of the governed, --That whenever any Form of Government becomes destructive of these ends, it is the Right of the People to alter or to abolish it, and to institute new Government, laying its foundation on such principles and organizing its powers in such form, as to them shall seem most likely to affect their Safety and Happiness.

We establish governments to provide for our security as a society. These governments get their powers from the citizens (not the other way around). At any time that the government becomes a threat to the citizen's rights, it is the *God given right* of the people to either change or completely abolish that government; it is then the duty of the people to form a new government to protect the safety and happiness of the nation.

Prudence, indeed, will dictate that Governments long established should not be changed for light and transient causes; and accordingly all experience hath shewn, that mankind are more disposed to suffer, while evils are sufferable, than to right themselves by abolishing the forms to which they are accustomed. But when a long train of abuses and usurpations, pursuing invariably the same Object evinces a design to reduce them under absolute Despotism, it is their right, it is their duty, to throw off such Government, and to provide new Guards for their future security.

Another self explanatory section, it basically says that we should not endeavor to overthrow a long standing government for frivolous reasons. However, when the government continuously abuses the people, stripping them of their liberties, etc. it is not only the people's right, but it is also their duty to overthrow that government, and form a new one.

Such has been the patient sufferance of these Colonies; and such is now the necessity which constrains them to alter their former Systems of Government. The history of the present King of Great Britain is a history of repeated injuries and usurpations, all having in direct object the establishment of an absolute Tyranny over these States. To prove this, let Facts be submitted to a candid world.

Here, and in the following segment, the authors begin to lay out the reasons for America's succession from Great Britain. They list the reasons in detail, so that the world at large will understand the necessity of their actions. Those reasons, or causes, are:

He has refused his Assent to Laws, the most wholesome and necessary for the public good.
He has forbidden his Governors to pass Laws of immediate and pressing importance, unless suspended in their operation till his Assent should be obtained; and when so suspended, he has utterly neglected to attend to them.
He has refused to pass other Laws for the accommodation of large districts of people, unless those people would relinquish the right of Representation in the Legislature, a right inestimable to them and formidable to tyrants only.
He has called together legislative bodies at places unusual, uncomfortable, and distant from the depository of their public Records, for the sole purpose of fatiguing them into compliance with his measures.
He has dissolved Representative Houses repeatedly, for opposing with manly firmness his invasions on the rights of the people.
He has refused for a long time, after such dissolutions, to

cause others to be elected; whereby the Legislative powers, incapable of Annihilation, have returned to the People at large for their exercise; the State remaining in the mean time exposed to all the dangers of invasion from without, and convulsions within.

He has endeavoured to prevent the population of these States; for that purpose obstructing the Laws for Naturalization of Foreigners; refusing to pass others to encourage their migrations hither, and raising the conditions of new Appropriations of Lands.

He has obstructed the Administration of Justice, by refusing his Assent to Laws for establishing Judiciary powers.

He has made Judges dependent on his Will alone, for the tenure of their offices, and the amount and payment of their salaries.

He has erected a multitude of New Offices, and sent hither swarms of Officers to harass our people, and eat out their substance.

He has kept among us, in times of peace, Standing Armies without the Consent of our legislatures.

He has affected to render the Military independent of and superior to the Civil power.

He has combined with others to subject us to a jurisdiction foreign to our constitution, and unacknowledged by our laws; giving his Assent to their Acts of pretended Legislation:

For Quartering large bodies of armed troops among us:

For protecting them, by a mock Trial, from punishment for any Murders which they should commit on the Inhabitants of these States:

For cutting off our Trade with all parts of the world:

For imposing Taxes on us without our Consent:

For depriving us in many cases, of the benefits of Trial by

Jury:

For transporting us beyond Seas to be tried for pretended offences

For abolishing the free System of English Laws in a neighbouring Province, establishing therein an Arbitrary government, and enlarging its Boundaries so as to render it at once an example and fit instrument for introducing the same absolute rule into these Colonies:

For taking away our Charters, abolishing our most valuable Laws, and altering fundamentally the Forms of our Governments:

For suspending our own Legislatures, and declaring themselves invested with power to legislate for us in all cases whatsoever.

He has abdicated Government here, by declaring us out of his Protection and waging War against us.

He has plundered our seas, ravaged our Coasts, burnt our towns, and destroyed the lives of our people.

He is at this time transporting large Armies of foreign Mercenaries to compleat the works of death, desolation and tyranny, already begun with circumstances of Cruelty & perfidy scarcely paralleled in the most barbarous ages, and totally unworthy the Head of a civilized nation.

He has constrained our fellow Citizens taken Captive on the high Seas to bear Arms against their Country, to become the executioners of their friends and Brethren, or to fall themselves by their Hands.

He has excited domestic insurrections amongst us, and has endeavoured to bring on the inhabitants of our frontiers, the merciless Indian Savages, whose known rule of warfare, is an undistinguished destruction of all ages, sexes and conditions.

In every stage of these Oppressions We have Petitioned for Redress in the most humble terms: Our repeated Petitions have been answered only by repeated injury. A Prince whose character is thus marked by every act which may define a Tyrant, is unfit to be the ruler of a free people.

Nor have We been wanting in attentions to our Brittish brethren. We have warned them from time to time of attempts by their legislature to extend an unwarrantable jurisdiction over us. We have reminded them of the circumstances of our emigration and settlement here. We have appealed to their native justice and magnanimity, and we have conjured them by the ties of our common kindred to disavow these usurpations, which, would inevitably interrupt our connections and correspondence. They too have been deaf to the voice of justice and of consanguinity. We must, therefore, acquiesce in the necessity, which denounces our Separation, and hold them, as we hold the rest of mankind, Enemies in War, in Peace Friends.

In these paragraphs, we find near parallels to our current state of affairs. We the people have petitioned for redress of the government usurpations of our liberties, but our petitions have fallen on deaf ears, both in government and in, some cases, among our fellow Americans. We say fellow Americans because there are some among us who believe that more government is what we need. However, like our founding fathers, we believe that people of this character have no right to rule over, or govern us. We are a free people. Men and women have fought and died for many generations to ensure that we were able to remain a free people. It is our duty now, as it was their duty then, to guard that freedom, and all that we hold dear, from the wolves at the door.

We, therefore, the Representatives of the united States of America, in General Congress, Assembled, appealing to the Supreme Judge of the world for the rectitude of our intentions, do, in the Name, and by Authority of the good People of these Colonies, solemnly publish and declare, That these United Colonies are, and of Right ought to be Free and Independent States; that they are Absolved from all Allegiance to the British Crown, and that all political connection between them and the State of Great Britain, is and ought to be totally dissolved; and that as Free and Independent States, they have full Power to levy War, conclude Peace, contract Alliances, establish Commerce, and to do all other Acts and Things which Independent States may of right do. And for the support of this Declaration, with a firm reliance on the protection of divine Providence, we mutually pledge to each other our Lives, our Fortunes and our sacred Honor.

This is, in our opinion, the most important paragraph in this document. It states that, after appealing to God to search their intentions, they are moved to publish and declare the thirteen colonies as Free states, no longer owing allegiance to the British Crown. Most importantly, they recognized the work of Divine Providence in the founding of this country. Furthermore, they pledged to each other everything that they had, and everything that they were, in supporting their Declaration of Independence. This is a pledge that we need to renew. A pledge that each of us, as Americans, need to make to one another.

The Constitution

This segment features selected portions of the Constitution of the United States. We have chosen to do only selected portions, because the entire document takes up twenty plus pages. We will cover only those sections that are of the utmost importance at this moment. There will be no commentary on this document. It speaks for itself. We do, however, recommend that you get a copy and read it for yourself.

We the People of the United States, in Order to form a more perfect Union, establish Justice, insure domestic Tranquility, provide for the common defense, promote the general Welfare, and secure the Blessings of Liberty to ourselves and our Posterity, do ordain and establish this Constitution for the United States of America.

Article. I.

Section. 1.

All legislative Powers herein granted shall be vested in a Congress of the United States, which shall consist of a Senate and House of Representatives.

Section. 2.

The House of Representatives shall be composed of Members chosen every second Year by the People of the several States, and the Electors in each State shall have the Qualifications requisite for Electors of the most numerous Branch of the State Legislature.

No Person shall be a Representative who shall not have attained to the Age of twenty five Years, and been seven Years a Citizen of the United States, and who shall not, when elected, be an Inhabitant of that State in which he shall be chosen.

The actual Enumeration shall be made within three Years after the first Meeting of the Congress of the United States, and within every subsequent Term of ten Years, in such Manner as they shall by Law direct. The Number of Representatives shall not exceed one for every thirty Thousand, but each State shall have at Least one Representative;

The House of Representatives shall choose their Speaker and other Officers; and shall have the sole Power of Impeachment.

Section. 3.

The Senate of the United States shall be composed of two Senators from each State, thereof for six Years; and each Senator shall have one Vote.

Immediately after they shall be assembled in Consequence of the first Election, they shall be divided as equally as may be into three Classes. The Seats of the Senators of the first Class shall be vacated at the Expiration of the second Year, of the second Class at the Expiration of the fourth Year, and of the third Class at the Expiration of the sixth Year, so that one third may be chosen every second Year;

No Person shall be a Senator who shall not have attained to the Age of thirty Years, and been nine Years a Citizen of the United States, and who shall not, when elected, be an Inhabitant of that State for which he shall be chosen.

The Vice President of the United States shall be President of the Senate, but shall have no Vote, unless they be equally divided.

The Senate shall choose their other Officers, and also a President pro tempore, in the Absence of the Vice President, or when he shall exercise the Office of President of the United States.

The Senate shall have the sole Power to try all Impeachments. When sitting for that Purpose, they shall be on Oath or Affirmation. When the President of the United States is tried, the Chief Justice shall preside: And no Person shall be convicted without the Concurrence of two thirds of the Members present.

Judgment in Cases of Impeachment shall not extend further than to removal from Office, and disqualification to hold and enjoy any Office of honor, Trust or Profit under the United States: but the Party convicted shall nevertheless be liable and subject to Indictment, Trial, Judgment and Punishment, according to Law.

Section. 4.

The Congress shall assemble at least once in every Year, and such Meeting shall be on the first Monday in December,(this section has since been amended) unless they shall by Law appoint a different Day.

Section. 5.

Each House shall keep a Journal of its Proceedings, and from time to time publish the same, excepting such Parts as may in their Judgment require Secrecy; and the Yeas and Nays of the Members of either House on any question shall, at the Desire of one fifth of those Present, be entered on the Journal.

Neither House, during the Session of Congress, shall, without the Consent of the other, adjourn for more than three days, nor to any other Place than that in which the two Houses shall be sitting.

Section. 6.

No Senator or Representative shall, during the Time for which he was elected, be appointed to any civil Office under the Authority of the United States, which shall have been created, or the Emoluments whereof shall have been increased during such time; and no Person holding any Office under the United States, shall be a Member of either House during his Continuance in Office.

Section. 7.

All Bills for raising Revenue shall originate in the House of Representatives; but the Senate may propose or concur with Amendments as on other Bills.

Every Bill which shall have passed the House of Representatives and the Senate, shall, before it become a Law, be presented to the President of the United States: If he approve he shall sign it, but if not he shall return it, with his Objections to that House in which it shall have originated, who shall enter the Objections at large on their

Journal, and proceed to reconsider it. If after such Reconsideration two thirds of that House shall agree to pass the Bill, it shall be sent, together with the Objections, to the other House, by which it shall likewise be reconsidered, and if approved by two thirds of that House, it shall become a Law. But in all such Cases the Votes of both Houses shall be determined by yeas and Nays, and the Names of the Persons voting for and against the Bill shall be entered on the Journal of each House respectively. If any Bill shall not be returned by the President within ten Days (Sundays excepted) after it shall have been presented to him, the Same shall be a Law, in like Manner as if he had signed it, unless the Congress by their Adjournment prevent its Return, in which Case it shall not be a Law.

Every Order, Resolution, or Vote to which the Concurrence of the Senate and House of Representatives may be necessary (except on a question of Adjournment) shall be presented to the President of the United States; and before the Same shall take Effect, shall be approved by him, or being disapproved by him, shall be repassed by two thirds of the Senate and House of Representatives, according to the Rules and Limitations prescribed in the Case of a Bill.

Section. 8.

The Congress shall have Power To lay and collect Taxes, Duties, Imposts and Excises, to pay the Debts and provide for the common Defence and general Welfare of the United States; but all Duties, Imposts and Excises shall be uniform throughout the United States;

To declare War, grant Letters of Marque and Reprisal, and make Rules concerning Captures on Land and Water;

To raise and support Armies, but no Appropriation of Money to that Use shall be for a longer Term than two Years;

To provide and maintain a Navy;

To make Rules for the Government and Regulation of the land and naval Forces;

To provide for calling forth the Militia to execute the Laws of the Union, suppress Insurrections and repel Invasions;

To provide for organizing, arming, and disciplining, the Militia, and for governing such Part of them as may be employed in the Service of the United States, reserving to the States respectively, the Appointment of the Officers, and the Authority of training the Militia according to the discipline prescribed by Congress;

To make all Laws which shall be necessary and proper for carrying into Execution the foregoing Powers, and all other Powers vested by this Constitution in the Government of the United States, or in any Department or Officer thereof.

Section. 9.

The Privilege of the Writ of Habeas Corpus shall not be suspended, unless when in Cases of Rebellion or Invasion the public Safety may require it.

No Bill of Attainder or ex post facto Law shall be passed.

No Title of Nobility shall be granted by the United States: And no Person holding any Office of Profit or Trust under them, shall, without the Consent of the Congress, accept of any present, Emolument, Office, or Title, of any kind whatever, from any King, Prince, or foreign State.

Article. II.

Section. 1.

The executive Power shall be vested in a President of the United States of America. He shall hold his Office during the Term of four Years, and, together with the Vice President, chosen for the same Term, be elected, as follows:

Each State shall appoint, in such Manner as the Legislature thereof may direct, a Number of Electors, equal to the whole Number of Senators and Representatives to which the State may be entitled in the Congress: but no Senator or Representative, or Person holding an Office of Trust or Profit under the United States, shall be appointed an Elector.

The Congress may determine the Time of choosing the Electors, and the Day on which they shall give their Votes; which Day shall be the same throughout the United States.

No Person except a natural born Citizen, or a Citizen of the United States, at the time of the Adoption of this Constitution, shall be eligible to the Office of President; neither shall any Person be eligible to that Office who shall not have attained to the Age of thirty five Years, and been fourteen Years a Resident within the United States.

The President shall, at stated Times, receive for his Services, a Compensation, which shall neither be increased nor diminished during the Period for which he shall have been elected, and he shall not receive within that Period any other Emolument from the United States, or any of them.

Before he enter on the Execution of his Office, he shall take the following Oath or Affirmation:--"I do solemnly swear (or affirm) that I will faithfully execute the Office of President of the United States, and will to the best of my Ability, preserve, protect and defend the Constitution of the United States."

Section. 2.

The President shall be Commander in Chief of the Army and Navy of the United States, and of the Militia of the several States, when called into the actual Service of the United States; he may require the Opinion, in writing, of the principal Officer in each of the executive Departments, upon any Subject relating to the Duties of their respective Offices, and he shall have Power to grant Reprieves and Pardons for Offences against the United States, except in Cases of Impeachment.

He shall have Power, by and with the Advice and Consent of the Senate, to make Treaties, provided two thirds of the Senators present concur; and he shall nominate, and by and with the Advice and Consent of the Senate, shall appoint Ambassadors, other public Ministers and Consuls, Judges of the supreme Court, and all other Officers of the United States, whose Appointments are not herein otherwise provided for, and which shall be established by Law: but the Congress may by Law vest the Appointment of such inferior Officers, as they think proper, in the President alone, in the Courts of Law, or in the Heads of Departments.

The President shall have Power to fill up all Vacancies that may happen during the Recess of the Senate, by granting Commissions which shall expire at the End of their next Session.

Section. 3.

He shall from time to time give to the Congress Information of the State of the Union, and recommend to their Consideration such Measures as he shall judge necessary and expedient; he may, on extraordinary Occasions, convene both Houses, or either of them, and in Case of Disagreement between them, with Respect to the Time of Adjournment, he may adjourn them to such Time as he shall think proper; he shall receive Ambassadors and other public Ministers; he shall take Care that the Laws be faithfully executed, and shall Commission all the Officers of the United States.

Section. 4.

The President, Vice President and all civil Officers of the United States, shall be removed from Office on Impeachment for, and Conviction of, Treason, Bribery, or other high Crimes and Misdemeanors.

Article III.

The Trial of all Crimes, except in Cases of Impeachment, shall be by Jury; and such Trial shall be held in the State where the said Crimes shall have been committed; but when not committed within any State, the Trial shall be at such Place or Places as the Congress may by Law have directed.

Section. 3.

Treason against the United States, shall consist only in levying War against them, or in adhering to their Enemies, giving them Aid and Comfort. No Person shall be convicted of Treason unless on the Testimony of two Witnesses to the same overt Act, or on Confession in open Court.

The Congress shall have Power to declare the Punishment of Treason, but no Attainder of Treason shall work Corruption of Blood, or Forfeiture except during the Life of the Person attainted.

Article. IV.

Section. 2.

The Citizens of each State shall be entitled to all Privileges and Immunities of Citizens in the several States.

A Person charged in any State with Treason, Felony, or other Crime, who shall flee from Justice, and be found in another State, shall on Demand of the executive Authority of the State from which he fled, be delivered up, to be removed to the State having Jurisdiction of the Crime.

The Congress shall have Power to dispose of and make all needful Rules and Regulations respecting the Territory or other Property belonging to the United States; and nothing in this Constitution shall be so construed as to Prejudice any Claims of the United States, or of any particular State.

Section. 4.

The United States shall guarantee to every State in this Union a Republican Form of Government, and shall protect each of them against Invasion; and on Application of the Legislature, or of the Executive (when the Legislature cannot be convened), against domestic Violence.

Article. V.

The Congress, whenever two thirds of both Houses shall deem it necessary, shall propose Amendments to this Constitution, or, on the Application of the Legislatures of two thirds of the several States, shall call a Convention for proposing Amendments, which, in either Case, shall be valid to all Intents and Purposes, as Part of this Constitution, when ratified by the Legislatures of three fourths of the several States, or by Conventions in three fourths thereof, as the one or the other Mode of Ratification may be proposed by the Congress; Provided that no Amendment which may be made prior to the Year One thousand eight hundred and eight shall in any Manner affect the first and fourth Clauses in the Ninth Section of the first Article; and that no State, without its Consent, shall be deprived of its equal Suffrage in the Senate.

This Constitution, and the Laws of the United States which shall be made in Pursuance thereof; and all Treaties made, or which shall be made, under the Authority of the United States, shall be the supreme Law of the Land; and the Judges in every State shall be bound thereby, any Thing in the Constitution or Laws of any State to the Contrary notwithstanding.

The Senators and Representatives before mentioned, and the Members of the several State Legislatures, and all executive and judicial Officers, both of the United States and of the several States, shall be bound by Oath or Affirmation, to support this Constitution; but no religious Test shall ever be required as a Qualification to any Office or public Trust under the United States.

Article. VII.

The Ratification of the Conventions of nine States, shall be sufficient for the Establishment of this Constitution between the States so ratifying the Same.

Done in Convention by the Unanimous Consent of the States present the Seventeenth Day of September in the Year of our Lord one thousand seven hundred and Eighty seven and of the Independence of the United States of America the Twelfth In witness whereof We have hereunto subscribed our Names,

Bill Of Rights:

This letter is simply a breakdown of our Bill of Rights. You know, those "negative rights" that President Obama refers to? Yeah, those.

Amendment I

Congress shall make no law respecting an establishment of religion, or prohibiting the free exercise thereof; or abridging the freedom of speech, or of the press; or the right of people to peaceably assemble, and to petition the government for a redress of grievances.

First and foremost, Congress cannot deem any religion as a national religion or prohibit the practice any specific religion. This means they cannot pass any laws that would make certain religious sects or denominations illegal. This is for those of you seeking to ban Christianity from our country. Our founders came here as Christians and based the majority of our laws on Christian law. To remove Christianity completely would be tantamount to denying our great country's history. Regarding freedom of speech, you have the right to say or print your opinions without worry of our government demonizing you. Also, those of us who belong to the "Astroturf" movement, as Nancy Pelosi so fondly refer to us, have the right to *peaceably* assemble at our town hall meetings, rallies, and tea parties as we see fit without worry of repercussions.

Amendment II

A well regulated militia, being necessary to the security of a free state, the right of the people to keep and bear arms, shall not be infringed.

This is the one that the progressives are constantly trying to abolish. We the people have the Right to keep *and* bear arms. For those who say that this right pertains only to law enforcement and the military, here are a few quotes from our founding fathers.

"Arms discourage and keep the invader and plunderer in awe, and preserve order in the world as well as property... Horrid mischief would ensue were the law-abiding deprived of the use of them." Thomas Paine. *"No free man shall ever be debarred the use of arms."* Thomas Jefferson. Then there is our personal favorite, "The strongest reason for the people to retain the right to keep and bear arms is, as a last resort, to protect themselves against tyranny in government." Thomas Jefferson.

Amendment III

No soldier shall, in time of peace be quartered in any house, without the consent of the owner, nor in time of war, but in a manner to be prescribed by law.

The third amendment is very simple. All it means is that the government cannot commandeer your house for the purpose of housing soldiers during peace time, and only as stated by law during war time.

Amendment IV

The right of the people to be secure in their persons, houses, papers, and effects, against unreasonable searches and seizures, shall not be violated, and no warrants shall issue, but upon probable cause, supported by oath or affirmation, and particularly describing the place to be searched, and the persons or things to be seized.

Amendment number four is very important, because it protects us from illegal search and seizure of private property. If it were not for this amendment, any government agent could, at any time, and for any reason, search and seize our property, and us. (This also goes back to the wiretapping of phones owned by people who were known to associate and communicate with terrorists. Those law enforcement agencies were required to have warrants, therefore making those legal.)

Amendment V

No person shall be held to answer for a capital, or otherwise infamous crime, unless on a presentment or indictment of a grand jury, except in cases arising in the land or naval forces, or in the militia, when in actual service in time of war or public danger; nor shall any person be subject for the same offense to be twice put in jeopardy of life or limb; nor shall be compelled in any criminal case to be a witness against himself, nor be deprived of life, liberty, or property, without due process of law; nor shall private property be taken for public use, without just compensation.

This amendment is commonly referred to as simply "double jeopardy". It means that you cannot be tried for any criminal charge, unless you are first indicted by a grand jury. You cannot be tried twice for the same crime if the jury in your case reaches a verdict, unless the prosecution obtains new evidence of your guilt. You cannot be made to make any incriminating statements against yourself. Last but not least, the government cannot take your property for public use without compensating you.

"No power on earth has a right to take our property from us without our consent." John Jay.

Amendment VI

In all criminal prosecutions, the accused shall enjoy the right to a speedy and public trial, by an impartial jury of the state and district wherein the crime shall have been committed, which district shall have been previously ascertained by law, and to be informed of the nature and cause of the

accusation; to be confronted with the witnesses
against him; to have compulsory process for
obtaining witnesses in his favor, and to have the
assistance of counsel for his defense.

Here, persons accused of any crime are given certain protections: the right to a speedy *and* public trial, the right to a trial by impartial jury, the right to be informed of the charges against you, confront the accuser, and have an attorney to defend you.

Amendment VII

In suits at common law, where the value in
controversy shall exceed twenty dollars, the right
of trial by jury shall be preserved, and no fact tried
by a jury, shall be otherwise reexamined in any
court of the United States, than according to the
rules of the common law.

In civil cases where the contested issue exceeds twenty dollars in value, you have the right to a jury trial. Once a case has been tried in court, no other court may re-examine the case, except in instances specifically outlined by law.

Amendment VIII

Excessive bail shall not be required, nor excessive
fines imposed, nor cruel and unusual punishments
inflicted.

This amendment protects those accused of any crime from unreasonable fines, and cruel and unusual punishment. Pretty self explanatory.

Amendment IX

The enumeration in the Constitution, of certain rights, shall not be construed to deny or disparage others retained by the people.

The fact that certain rights are covered in specificity in the Constitution does not, in any way, take away from any other rights retained by the people.

Amendment X

The powers not delegated to the United States by the Constitution, nor prohibited by it to the states, are reserved to the states respectively, or to the people.

This amendment is very important. It specifically designates *all powers not assigned* to the Federal government or prohibited *by the Constitution*, to the individual states.

Now that you are aware of the rights given to us by our founders, it is your job to protect and preserve them.

Chapter 4

Elected Officials.

Have they forgotten who elected them?

"Guard against the impostures of pretended patriotism."

George Washington

"When a man assumes a public trust he should consider himself a public property."

Thomas Jefferson

America: It's NOT a Democracy!

What? Did we say that right? Yep, sure did. It's not a democracy. It is a Republic. It was set up as a Republic. The founding fathers found Democracy repulsive. Why? Democracy is the twin to socialism. You doubt us? Read the chapter on our founding documents. Instead of trying to explain it again, we'll let the men who wrote that great document to explain. Here are a few quotes that illustrate exactly how those men felt. We'll leave you to interpret these remarks for yourself.

"The republican is the only form of government which is not eternally at open or secret war with the rights of mankind." Thomas Jefferson.
"Government is not reason; it is not eloquent; it is force. Like fire, it is a dangerous servant and a fearful master." George Washington.
"Democracy… while it lasts is more bloody than either aristocracy or monarchy. Remember, democracy never lasts long. It soon wastes, exhausts, and murders itself. There is never a democracy that did not commit suicide." John Adams.

The list goes on. If we did nothing but quote the founding fathers on this subject, this letter would be several pages long. Nancy's favorite quote, though, is the following: "Do not separate text from historical background. If you do, you will have perverted and subverted the Constitution, which can only end in a distorted, bastardized form of illegitimate government." James Madison. That pretty much says it all, doesn't it?

Our founders worked hard, laboring over our Constitution and the formation of our government. They knew that, if this country was to have a chance to survive, we had to have the right government. One that was strong enough to protect the citizens, and stand the test of time, yet weak enough to not pose a threat to liberty. That is certainly not what we have today. We have allowed the perversion and subversion of our Constitution. We have allowed power hungry individuals to corrupt our government to the point that our founders would not recognize it as their creation. If Mr. Madison was right, with what does that leave us? You decide.

For your convenience, we looked up the definitions of both words; democracy and republic.

Webster's defines a democracy as:

1.) Government by the people, directly or through representatives
2.) A country, etc. with such a government
3.) Equality of rights, opportunity, and treatment.

The word Republic is defined as:

A state or government, specifically one headed by a president, in which the power is exercised by officials elected by the voters.

See the difference? It is a subtle, but powerful one, we assure you. For the sake of comparison, we also looked up another word: socialism... it is defined as:

political system of communal ownership: a political theory or system in which the means of production and distribution are controlled by the people and operated according to equity and fairness rather than market principles.

Now you know where our country is headed. Don't say we didn't warn you. What's worse is that we aren't the only ones. Glenn Beck, Sean Hannity, Rush Limbaugh, Bill O'Reilly, and many others tried to tell us it was coming to this. Unfortunately, we all seem to have taken melatonin, because we never even opened our eyes. We just snoozed right through it. We just hope that the melatonin wears off before our country becomes the EU part 2.

Congressional Contracts

A wise man once said, "All that is required for evil to triumph, is for good men to do nothing". We humbly submit that this axiom can be directly applied to our current national situation, with, perhaps, a slight bit of rewording. So instead it would read, "All that is required for tyranny to triumph, is for patriots to do nothing." Yeah, we like the sound of that. Make no mistake, ladies and gentlemen; we are fighting a war against tyranny. Daily, those despots in Washington, and even in our own state capitals, pass laws that strip innocent, law abiding citizens of a little more of their liberty. They say that these laws are for the good of the community, state, and /or nation. This is an outright lie! Very few, if any, of those jackals actually care what is good for the citizenry of this country. They care about lining their own pockets and getting re-elected. This is evidenced by the continual passing of laws that aid special interest groups and lobbyists in whatever pet projects they may have, while hurting the citizens. This cannot be allowed to continue! Our elected officials are supposed to be working for us. Were these kinds of actions taking place in the private sector, we would sue them for breach of contract.

In fact, that might not be such a bad idea. Hmm. We should make our representatives, congressmen, senators, etc. sign contracts stating what they are obligated to do on our behalf, and prohibiting them from passing any laws or bills that work against the interest of their constituency. Then, when they mess up, we would at least have some course by which we could address these grievances. In fact, that does happen on the local level. Also included in these contracts would be a morality clause. Why? It's simple; if these men and women are responsible for running our country, they should be held to a higher standard of morality. Take for instance our armed forces. In the military, fraternization and adultery are illegal, punishable by court marshal and up to two years in a federal prison. These people, who are constantly in the public eye, should be held to the same level of accountability. We are so sick of hearing about this mayor, or that senator, cheating on his wife, cheating on their taxes, committing rape, murder, or manslaughter, going on some drunken or drug induced binge, or being caught in various scandals such as soliciting sex from homosexual deviants. Yes, you know who we're talking about. We should not have to list names.

It is true what they say: "Power corrupts, and absolute power corrupts absolutely." That statement is proven by the fact that we have career politicians, who have never held an actual job in their lifetimes, running our country. In fact, they are not just running our country! They are running the banking, transportation, food, and healthcare, and many more sectors as well. These people have no idea how to run a business, and they are now in charge of the four largest private sector industries in the nation! How did this happen? Thomas Paine said it best. "When the people fear the government, you have tyranny. When the government fears the people, you have liberty."

Personally, we're beginning to believe that the majority of US citizens suffer from Attention Deficit Disorder. It's like, "This is a travesty! We have to do some...Oh look!

Something shiny..." We don't pay attention to the news long enough to figure out that our country is in jeopardy. And what little news we do engage in is twisted to fit the agenda of a biased media. We don't realize that liberty and freedom are under attack, not from any outside source, but from the very people who we put in office to protect those ideas. Adolf Hitler stated "How fortunate for governments that the people they administer don't think." We cannot let this stand! If we sit idly by while they strip away the very freedoms that our forefathers and ancestors fought so hard to obtain, then we deserve what we get!

Our children don't deserve it. Our children deserve to grow up in the same free America that we grew up in. They deserve to be afforded the same opportunities that we were. They deserve to be able to choose for themselves. We owe it to them to preserve the proud heritage of this great nation. We owe it to our children to make sure that they have the freedom to make the decisions that will affect their futures. It is not our place to rob our children of the same liberties that we enjoyed.

America's Transformers: <u>More Than Meets The Eye</u>

Over the last seven months, we Americans have become increasingly upset about the changes taking place in our country, and indeed, our government. It seems that we neglected to recognize what was right in front of our eyes. Americans have always said that we want honest politicians, who would tell us up front, who they are, what they stand for, and what they want to do for the country.

Unfortunately for us, we have grown so used to politicians lying to us, that we failed to see the fact that this one was, indeed, telling the truth. We didn't take Mr. Obama seriously when he told us, before and after the election, what he wanted to do to this nation. He never hid behind a facade, the way people claim. No, he let us know up front, what he was going to do if he was elected. Now we have the nerve to be upset that he is keeping his word.

"We are five days away from fundamentally transforming the United States of America." "It's not that I want to punish your success. I just want to make sure that everybody who is behind you, that they've got a chance at success, too. I think when you spread the wealth around, it's good for everybody." Barack Obama.

Obama also wants an expanded civil service type organization. He said, "We cannot continue to rely only on our military in order to achieve the national security objectives that we've set. We've got to have a civilian national security force that's just as powerful, just as strong, just as well funded." When asked about this, Rahm Emanuel had this to say:

VOICE: The idea of universal citizen's service, [is that] you have to participate.
EMANUEL: Citizenship is not an entitlement program. It comes with responsibilities. Everybody somewhere between the ages of 18 and 25 will serve three months of basic training in a kind of civil defense. That universal sense of service, somewhere between ages 18 and 25 will give Americans once again a sense of what they are to be American and their contribution to a country and a common experience. And you look at World War II. That was a draft. This is not a draft. It's a universal service. It is not an accident that we started our big march towards civil rights and expanding post World War II because the country came through and experienced together.
VOICE: So is this compulsory then?
EMANUEL: Well, you have to in a sense that it's required of everybody.

Yes, you read that right, mandated civil service for all US citizens aged 18 to 25. Now, some would say that such a policy is reminiscent of Nazi Germany's policy of mandated youth service. Not us, we think that everyone should be in service to the new regime. Really, who wouldn't want to be part of a wonderful, brave new world? A world in which there are no more evil rich corporations, and rich white men making all the laws. We need more radical black nationalists, avowed communists, and anti-capitalists running the country. Really, and anyone who doesn't agree with the agenda should be immediately rounded up and placed in internment camps. While in those camps, dissidents should be tortured and brainwashed until they fully committed to furthering the agenda of the new regime. Don't you agree?

But we digress. The point is that America voted for the warm fuzzy feeling that this man's oratory prowess gave us, instead of actually listening to what he had to say. We looked to a mere human being to bring us "hope and change," instead of looking to ourselves to change the way things are. Now we are paying the price for being uninformed and uneducated. America, it is time that we stop trusting the men and women in Washington to represent our best interests. We have to start educating ourselves, and making sure that our elected officials represent the will of their constituents. We have to vote our consciences instead of toeing the party line. Most importantly, when those who are elected to represent us do what is contrary to the best interests of the nation, we have got to hold their collective feet to the fire. We have to make sure that they are aware of the consequences of their actions.

It is no longer acceptable to allow them carte blanche to do as they wish. It is no longer alright to let them disregard our wishes in lieu of what will put the most money in their private coffers. We elected them to do a job. It is their job to represent us, and when they mess up, it is our responsibility to call them on it. We need to remind them that they have an obligation to the American citizenry, and we need to do it now. If we wait, in the vain hope that things will get better, it will be too late.

This is one problem for which we have a solution. Voter Recall is the process that allows for an elected official's removal from office *during their term* by a vote of their constituency. Basically, it's a way to fire them. Unfortunately, only 18 states and the district of Columbia currently have legislation allowing this. These states are:

- Alaska
- Arizona
- California
- Colorado
- Georgia
- Idaho
- Kansas
- Louisiana
- Michigan
- Minnesota
- Montana
- Nevada
- New Jersey
- North Dakota
- Oregon
- Rhode Island
- Washington
- Wisconsin

(Virginia allows for a recall by trial instead of election.)
We propose a multilevel solution.

1. Write your senators and congressmen/women, and demand that the senate begin impeachment proceedings against President Obama.
2. If they refuse, look into your state's statutes for recall.
3. Begin the process of starting a voter recall.
4. If your state does not allow voter recall, demand that such legislation be introduced and enacted in your state senate.
5. Hold them responsible for their malfeasance!

We do not have to put up with their misconduct, and gross ineptitude. We do not have to wait until the next election to make them face the music. Do it now, before they pass any more legislation that encroaches on our freedom.

Do not let it be said that we lay down and let them walk all over us. We are not doormats! We are Americans! We have fought for liberty and freedom all over the world. Let's not neglect to fight for our own liberty and freedom.

"If a nation expects to be ignorant and free, in a state of civilization, it expects what never was and never will be." Thomas Jefferson.

Taxation Without Representation?

You tell me. Alexander Hamilton said, "In the main it will be found that a power over a man's support (salary) is a power over his will." Let's examine that statement. If power over a man's salary, or income, is power over his will where does that leave us? The government controls all of our incomes. They tell employers how much they have to pay us, and then they take a portion of it for their own usage. Do we stand up to them? No. Do we tell them we've had enough; that we will no longer abide these insane tax increases? No. We just bend over and take it. What happened to the spirit of America? What happened to the people who fought for their rights, and for the rights of others? Instead of being those people, we stick our heads in the sand, and "hope it will get better…" WAKE UP!!! It is our indifference, and refusal to hold these people accountable that has allowed things to go this far.

They are passing laws right and left that not only take our money, but also force small businesses to close their doors. They can no longer afford to operate because of the taxes they have to pay. Small business accounts for seventy percent of the jobs in this nation. Still wondering why unemployment continues to climb? This path is unsustainable. If we continue down this road, our country will never recover. We will go down in history as a failed experiment. Is that what you want?

One of the largest motivations behind the colonists' original stance against Britain was "Taxation without representation." Hmm. Let's explore that. They tax us half to death in order to fund programs and legislation that do not benefit us in any way, without bothering to ask what their constituency wants. Doesn't that mean that we are currently being taxed without representation? If so, what do you think we should do about it? Should we allow it to continue? You tell me. We're not here to incite you to violence, only to inspire you to think for yourself.

Small Victories

Fellow patriots,

Today we have some really good news. After quite a bit of disturbing information about Obama's "Green Jobs Czar" Van Jones, Mr. Jones tendered his resignation, effective immediately, over the Labor Day Weekend. This is a small victory for those of us who hold to our conservative values. We are excited about this turn of events, but we caution Americans to stay the course. This is only a minor victory. Mr. Jones, while he has exhibited deplorable beliefs, is only one of many such people who are part of the current administration. Let us not forget about Cass Sunstien, Rahm and Ezekiel Emmanuel, John Holdren and the others. They are just as radical as Van Jones is, and they still hold positions of power within our government. In our opinion, Mr. Jones was, in all likelihood, thrown under the bus due to his controversial statements.

Most of us are aware that these "czars" are unconstitutional. We know that these people have large amounts of power, and yet are completely outside the bounds of the law. They do not answer to anyone except the president, which is, in itself, unconstitutional. It has become increasingly apparent to most of us that the executive branch is expanding itself beyond the limits set by our constitution. It is devouring both of the other governmental branches in its hunger for power. So far, this process has been slow and insidious, but that fact does not detract from the reality of the situation.

Let us not forget that this administration had consistently tried to circumvent the legislative branch via the massive, unreadable bill that it continues to introduce into congress. By using supporters within the congress to sponsor the bills, they are able to eliminate the little inconvenience of congress members even writing the bills. Nowadays, legislative bills are being written by such special interest groups as the Apollo Alliance. How did that happen? When did our legislators decide it was better to delegate their responsibility to make legislation? Making legislation means more than just voting on the bills; it means writing the legislation, reading and making any needed changes, and then voting on it. It is meant to be a somewhat cumbersome, time consuming process. It was designed that way to prevent the very types of monstrously sweeping legislation that we are seeing today.

America, we cannot relax our vigilance in regards to this administration. They need us to relax and go back to sleep. They know that if we continue to be aware of their agenda, and stand up for our rights, then they will be unable to make any progress. That is the point. We have to make sure that they don't make any progress. Progress for them means abolishing all of the rights and freedoms that we, as Americans, have fought so hard to gain and preserve. We cannot allow it. We must stand firm in our resolve and resistance. It is our responsibility to make sure that our constitution remains intact. We have seen incontrovertible evidence that we can no longer trust our elected officials to stand for our values. We have to do that. We can no longer be complacent about our government. That complacency has led us into the disasters that we currently face. If we are to save our America, we have to take the responsibility of preserving it.

"Every government degenerates when trusted to the rulers of the people alone. The people themselves are its only safe depositories." Thomas Jefferson.

Chapter 5

Where We Are Today...And where we should be.

"Leave no authority existing not responsible to the people."

Thomas Jefferson

"I predict future happiness for Americans if they can prevent the government from wasting the labors of the people under the pretense of taking care of them."

Thomas Jefferson

America: The Fat Rich Kid

I had a conversation with my sister in law today that I found both humorous and true. We were discussing the fact that, while our government has spent the last several decades flushing this country down the toilet, we have done nothing to stop it. As sad as that is, it is exactly what has a happened and is happening. Our elected politicians have spent their careers lining their pockets and helping their buddies, the citizenry be damned. Jen's theory is that it has been allowed because America is like the fat rich kid. You know, the kid who has had everything handed to him, and has never had to work a day in his life. He doesn't appreciate what he has, and he never will, because he hasn't had to work for it.

We whine and cry about how bad our economy is, or how unemployment keeps rising. We talk about how we don't want socialized healthcare, and how the stimulus has failed. All this, and we don't actually _do_ anything. America, it is time for us to get up off the couch, go do something constructive, and stop whining. If we want "Hope & Change," it is up to us to make the changes that will give us hope. We can't leave it up to some suave politician with a glib tongue and ready rhetoric. Contrary to popular belief, he is not our savior.

Thomas Paine said it best, "He who dares not offend cannot be honest." Well, I have no problem with that. I'll be honest with you even if it makes you mad. Why? Because I care too much about this country, and the futures of our children, to shut my mouth and stand on the sidelines. I refuse to be silent in the face of tyranny. Someone has to stand up and say what everyone else is thinking. It might as well be me. We need to be reminded that only by standing up can we affect change. It's not going to happen otherwise. There are no genies with magic lamps waiting to grant our wishes. There is no magic formula that will make everything alright again. That will require work. However, it will be a moot point if we don't give voice to our discontent.

To quote another of our founding fathers, Thomas Jefferson said, "One man with courage is a majority." I agree whole heartedly with that sentiment. Words are a powerful weapon, that, when used properly, can move men to change the world. I guess that's what these letters are all about. I know that there are other people out there who feel the way that I do. I'm asking you all to stand up for the America that we all believe in; the America that you and I both love. America is bleeding. She lies beaten and broken in crumpled mass on the floor. What are we going to do now? Do we turn our backs to her pain, or do we pick her up, tend her wounds, and nurse her back to health? The choice is ours, and the decision is now. Tomorrow she may be dead.

"Public Schools"

Remember back when you were a kid, and you couldn't wait for school to start? You got to go to the store with your mom and pick out all your supplies. You were so excited because she let you pick out your notebooks, etc. We think those times are among the happiest memories that we have. We mean, we got to express who we were through our choices. For a kid, that's a big deal. The only thing that beat it was picking out our school clothes.

Do you realize that our kids don't get to have that experience, unless they go to private schools? We buy our children's school supplies based on a list that the school provides, but then their teacher puts all of that stuff into a community pot for those kids who are "less fortunate." The truth of the matter is, the majority of these children have parents who are just too darned lazy to go out and get a job. Funny thing is, we have observed that most of these "less fortunate" children wear name brand clothing (ie. Tommy Hilfiger, Ralph Lauren, Nike, etc.), and the parents who are "unable to provide" school supplies for their children, are driving either a Cadillac or a Lexus, or some other $50,000 vehicle. How is that fair, or right? It is not our responsibility to buy supplies for the other kids in our child's class. It is the responsibility of their parents. Our kids should not have to sacrifice the supplies that he or she picked out, so that some welfare kid's parents don't have to take responsibility for their child. It's ridiculous. We need to stop coddling and enabling these people. They will never have any incentive to do what's right, if we take care of all of their needs. When someone you love becomes addicted to some sort of drug, do you give them money to buy their drug of choice, or do you try to help them overcome their addiction? It's the same principle here. "Give a man a fish, and he'll eat for a day. Teach a man to fish, and he'll eat for a lifetime." People become addicted to letting the government take care of them, and never try to take care of themselves. What do you think the solution should be?

In addition to that, the education that our children receive is, at best, sub-prime. When a child can reach the age of graduation, without being able to read proficiently, count back change, or have any concept of cause and effect, something is wrong. Now the system is teaching our kids that grades don't matter. That all that is required is that they "try." For example, when my child was in first grade, about half way through the school year, her grades started slipping. Rather than the teacher trying to contact me, and figure out why, the school simply placed her in resource classes, and told her not to worry about it. We later found out that she had a visual impairment, which caused her to be unable to read the class material. Also, how long do you think it takes for the average kid to figure out that all they have to do is pretend to try? They are not doing any service to us or our children. In our opinion, they are deliberately "dumbing down" the next generation. Uneducated people are much easier to control than those who think for themselves. Don't you think? Don't let them turn our children into mindless sheep. Or they will be quietly led to the slaughter with no idea as to what's happening. It is true what they say, education does start at home, and it is our responsibility as parents to see that our children learn the things that they need to know in order to survive, and have the tools to do so.

"Universal education is the most corroding and disintegrating poison that liberalism has ever invented for its own destruction." Adolf Hitler.

ENTITLEMENT MENTALITY

Ever noticed how so many people now days think that everything is owed to them? I have, and it ticks me off. It is called entitlement mentality. It seems that this trend is growing. Young adults and teens seem to suffer from this the most. I blame the parents and government. The television doesn't help matters either. But, that goes back to parenting. People no longer seem to think that they have to put in a hard day's work for anything. "Mom and Dad should buy the first car and pay for college." "Mom and Dad should pay my cell phone bill and give me money to go out on Friday nights." "The government should provide me with a house and my kids an education and food and health care and the internet." How many times have you heard someone say this? Truth is, you probably know someone personally who thinks this way.

The first time I noticed it was in the aftermath of Hurricane Katrina. Don't get me wrong; what happened to the people of New Orleans was tragic. A friend of mine was deployed to New Orleans 2 days after the hurricane struck. He spent 7 months dealing with the aftermath; getting shot at by civilians, gathering the dead, rescuing the living, and cleaning out the hospitals and houses, among other things. It was heartbreaking. Unfortunately, an underlying problem tainted the whole humanity of it all.

He has told me stories of people who would drive from unaffected parishes as far north as Baton Rouge in Cadillacs and Lexus' asking for a food handout and such. One story that bothered me a great deal was of a man who shot his own sister over a bag of ice in front of the young woman's child and others who were waiting in line to be assisted. Situations like this made it incredibly difficult to help those who truly needed it. For months, in the news, I heard of victims refusing to get jobs, demanding free boarding, and spending their FEMA money on things like big screen TVs and even a sex change. On top of all these stories, there were those of the destruction of private and public property. All of these events just left a bad taste in the mouths of those who were willing to give freely to help.

Another incident that bothered me greatly happened when my daughter was in kindergarten. The public school she went to had a "career day." The children were individually asked to stand up and tell what they would like to do when they grow up. Innocent and sweet, right? You would think , but, no. One particular young man stood up and voiced that he wanted to be just like his daddy. When asked what his daddy does, he promptly answered his daddy sits at home all day and watches TV and plays video games. He then stated that the government sends his daddy money once a month and buys their food. This sickened me. My daughter was distraught over why her "mommy wouldn't do that for her." Luckily, I took the opportunity to instill at that tender age of five the desire to strive for more and to take pride in doing so.

I grew up poor. A portion of my life was spent in government housing. There was even a summer that I lived in a motel, a loft room over stables, and then a tiny fifth wheel trailer with two adults in the parking lot of a restaurant where all three of us worked. I was uncomfortably aware of my thrift store clothes and that little booklet of brightly colored food stamps at a very early age. In my teen years, I went to live with an aunt and uncle where I learned an entirely new way of life. With five kids in the house and one meager income, we still had everything we needed and most of what we wanted. If we wanted more, we worked for it.

When I was fourteen, I cleaned stables for a friend's dad. I mowed yards, collected cans, participated in yard sales, did chores for neighbors, I even changed the oil in a few cars. I liked having the ability to buy a sweater that 'mom' wouldn't splurge for in the middle of the school year. I took pride in it. Granted, too much pride is a downfall. But I learned the value of earning something for myself, and I took better care of what I had. When it came time to get my first car, I bought it. My 'dad' then oversaw the tasks of rebuilding the carburetor and all the other necessary maintenance. As a reward for all my hard work, my parents bought me a new set of tires for my sixteenth birthday. I know this is not what most sixteen year old girls would want as a present, but I loved it. I was more grateful for that one thing and the lesson that went along with it than anything else I had ever received from them.

Why don't we teach our kids this lesson anymore? I try to with my children. Granted, I still have this nagging voice in the back of my head that tells me they should have more than I did. And they do. My oldest daughter knows the value of work though. She knows what it means to put in a hard days labor and take the money she earns and put it in her little brightly painted piggy bank for a rainy day. I have no worries that when the day comes for her to be on her own, she won't need "government help". She will be able to take care of herself and she will be happy to do so. She knows it's ok to ask for help when you truly need it, but she also knows not to depend on others to do it all for her. She knows that she is not entitled to anything but the God given freedom to make her own way is this life.

CJE

Chapter 6

Us Against Them?

"These are the times that try men's souls... Tyranny, like hell, is not easily conquered; yet we have this consolation with us, that the harder the conflict, the more glorious the triumph. What we obtain too cheaply, we esteem too lightly; 'tis dearness only that gives everything its value."
Thomas Paine

"The tree of liberty must be refreshed from time to time with the blood of patriots and tyrants."
Thomas Jefferson

Terrorists? Really????

Well, America, they've done it again!!! One of the senators from the great state of Florida, which, I'm almost ashamed to say is my home state, has introduced a bill that would label those of us who own/carry guns, believe in free speech, or think that government should be smaller, not bigger, terrorists. That's right folks; CJ and I are home grown terrorists according to this bill. In fact, you probably are, too. How does that make you feel? And it gets worse. Do you believe in Jesus Christ? If you said yes, you are an evil fundamentalist. Have you or any of your friends or loved ones ever served in the military? If so, you are automatically a suspected terrorist. What? You say you haven't done anything wrong? Have you not been paying attention? That doesn't matter anymore! All it takes for you to be labeled in this way is for the Attorney General to disagree with anything you say or do.

But wait, we're not finished yet! This same senator also introduced a bill, HR645, which would create what could essentially function as concentration or re-education camps for political dissidents. Look it up. Are we saying that this will happen? No. What we're saying is that it is a possibility. We're saying that if we stand by and allow our government carte blanche to label anyone a terrorist, and build these prison camps within our borders, we deserve what we get. After all, it has happened in this country before. Ask any Japanese American who lived here during WWII. In fact, look up the history of Ward Lake Park in Ketchikan, AK.

Now, please bear in mind, that the senator who proposed this bill is the same man who, in 1989, was a Federal Judge in Palm Beach County, and was impeached for perjury. Will someone please tell us how this guy got elected as a senator? Then again, most of our elected officials are crooks, so it shouldn't surprise us. But seriously, if this guy swung any farther to the left, he'd be hanging upside down! (Hmmm, that might not be a bad idea...) {And before anyone starts calling us racist, Nancy is half black. Just thought we'd let you know.} To make ourselves clear, we are *NOT* advocating violence.

What we don't get, is the fact that we, as American citizens, will sit idly on the side lines and let all of this take place with nary a hew or cry. What has happened to the independent, free spirit of the United States? Why are we sitting on our hands and not saying anything? We thought this was the land of the free. Whatever happened to that? We have gone from being a proud nation, willing to fight for freedom at any cost, to being a nation of sheeple who allow our government to think for us. When did that happen? Sometime during the last fifty years, we seem to have just given up and lain down. Why? Again, we are not trying to incite violence. There is such a thing as a peaceful resistance. We're just saying that we have to do something, and writing letters to our congressmen, senators, and representatives is no longer doing any good. However, The Constitution, on which this once great nation was built, gives us the tools to fight back.

That is why we propose that we choose a date, and have a "Back to the Basics" rally. The purpose of this rally to be to let our government officials know that we want them to return to the core of the Constitution. Our founding fathers wrote that great document as a core set of laws by which this country should be governed. It is not a "living document". It is what it is, and it's time we got back to it. Our representatives need to stop representing the Lobbyists and Special Interest groups, and start doing the jobs they were elected to do, by representing their constituency. We are so sick and tired of them passing laws and bills that go completely against the interests of the people just so that they can line their own pockets and earn favor with the SI groups. We need to remind these people that they are elected officials, and they can be voted out of office just as easily as we voted them in. It is passed time for them to step up to the plate and be what they represent themselves to be when they are campaigning for office. We say we pass a new law. Any elected official who fails to keep campaign promises, or runs on a conservative platform when they are actually liberal (or vice versa) should be fired. That's right; we should be able to fire them. We should not have to wait until their terms are completed. In any other business, if an employee fails to perform at the agreed upon standards, they can be terminated. Why can we not terminate government officials? Just a thought.

Like we said before, we don't know if any of things will actually happen, but no one thought it would really happen in Nazi Germany, either. Let's not forget that it was not only Jews who were sent to the concentration camps and murdered. It was also those who did not ascribe the Nazi regimes' beliefs and propaganda. It is time to take a stand, ladies and gentlemen. Don't make the mistake of believing that this will all go away. It won't, it will only get worse. Don't wait until we have no freedoms to get angry. Stop it before it gets to that point.

P.S. A little piece of trivia for you: The Nazis got their wonderful ideas for concentration camps and killing "undesirables" from us.

Liberty vs. Security

"Any society that would give up a little liberty to gain a little security will deserve neither and lose both."
Benjamin Franklin

That is a bold statement, and one that bears repeating. Yet, that is exactly what we, as Americans, are doing. We have allowed our government to run rampant, and done nothing to curb their insanity. We allowed the last president to pass a law, The Patriot Act, that gives the president the power to make himself a dictator, and are now allowing the current president to flush our economy down the drain. We may as well set our money on fire. We'll get about the same level of gratification.

We allow them to pass laws that regulate our ability to own firearms, like The Brady Bill. Now we have a new threat to that right, H.R. 45. (We want to know why. Law abiding citizens don't commit gun crimes, criminals do.) We let them tell us that our children have to go to public schools. We allowed legislation that keeps us from disciplining our children, as well. We let them tell us that smoking is bad, and should therefore be banned, and we even let them tell us that, by 2012, we have to use mercury filled light bulbs in our homes. What next??? We have allowed the government to dictate that we will have highly medicated, out of control children who will get a substandard education. However, thanks to the lawmakers, they won't be able to get guns. (I guess we should be grateful for that). Unfortunately, those of us who are law abiding citizens won't be able to get guns to protect our homes, property, and families from these out of control children who grow up to be out of control adults. We are expected use light bulbs that, should they break, require a hazmat team to clean up. Wanna know whose idea this was? Look no further than House Speaker Nancy Pelosi. For the sake of expedience, we'll withhold our personal opinion of her. The point is this: at what point do we get tired of this mess and stand up for ourselves? When do we say, "Enough!"? Or do we just continue to be sheeple who allow the politicians to do whatever they want to do? At what point did our governmental officials get to be above the law? Since when do laws that apply to everyone else, not apply to them? What gives them the right to pass legislation for "our benefit" when most of them have no experience living as a middle class American?

Ladies and gentlemen, citizens and patriots, we have got to do something to stop this insane recklessness. There is no reason in the world that our country should be in such dire straits, or that we as citizens should be losing our precious liberties. We cannot allow this to continue. We cannot leave it for our kids to deal with. If we do, our children won't have any liberties for which to fight.

Fear Mongering

"Delay is preferable to error." Thomas Jefferson. "Fear is the foundation of most governments." John Adams. Have you noticed lately that everything that the senate and congress are doing has to be done in a hurry? "If we don't act now, horrible things will happen!" They tell us they are acting quickly to save us all from catastrophe. This couldn't be further from the truth, Ladies and Gentlemen. The truth of the matter is that they use fear as an excuse to rush legislation that we would never agree to into law. If they are able to speed through the process without giving us the chance to read the bills they are passing, all the better. That is why they are overloading the system. Since Obama took office, there has constantly been one big story or another that the mainstream media latches onto, to the exclusion of all else. That means that we don't even hear about what they are doing, or if we do, it's after the bill has passed. Would you like to know why?

It really is very simple. Divide and conquer. They get us focused on one thing while they sneak something even worse through behind our backs. For instance, this healthcare bill that everyone is so wrapped up in. Understandably, we all are worried about this bill, as it would mean very bad things for the nation, economically. It would also mean the loss of many of our personal liberties and freedoms. The atrocities in this bill are for too many to number, and are sickening to even ponder. Besides which, we've covered it at length elsewhere in the book. This letter is about the other side of the coin, and no, we don't mean the benefits. There are none that we can discern.

No, this letter is about making sure that you are aware of this tactic and its daily use in the current congress and administration. It all goes back WMDs. If the system is overloaded, and we all concentrating on their latest gaff, or their latest moronic action, then we don't see the man holding the puppet strings. (What? You don't see the puppet strings? Look more carefully, they are made of fishing wire.) But seriously people, we have got to start paying attention. Like Glenn Beck said, don't try to concentrate on everything. Your head will explode. We are only capable of assimilating a certain amount of information. After that, our brains become mush. Instead, we should all find one thing to watch, and raise nine kinds if something changes. Let the rest of us know what's going on, because we are all watching something else. That way, there's less chance of these despots succeeding in turning this great nation into something we don't recognize.

If we can't come together and do this, then we deserve whatever happens. Personally, we think that America is better than that. We don't deserve to have our freedoms stripped, and our liberties lost. We are America. Strength, pride, freedom, and prosperity are our national heritage. Weakness, poverty, shame, and restriction are the antithesis of who we are, and as such, are and should be, abominations to us. It's time we remembered who we are. Stop lying down and playing lap dog. We are the defenders of freedom, the protectors of the weak, and the haven for those who cannot find comfort. We are, by nature, watch dogs. Let's return to that.

Let's go back to the proud nation we used to be. Let's stop acting like patriotism is a four letter word. There is nothing in the world wrong with being proud of our heritage. Don't let those who have no heritage to take pride in guilt us into feeling ashamed of ours. We are better than that, we have always been better than that, and if we have our way, we will always be better than that.

We ask you now to pledge to always hold our country in high esteem, to always and diligently defend and protect the rights, freedoms, and liberty that our ancestors fought, bled and died to give us. We pledge to you "our lives, our fortunes, and our sacred honor" to do the same.

"It is the duty of the patriot to protect his country from his government" Thomas Paine.

Chapter 7

Just For General Principles

"Enlighten the people generally, and tyranny and oppressions of body and mind will vanish like evil spirits at the dawn of day." Thomas Jefferson.

Control Your Children, Please!!!

Have you noticed that in recent years, children are becoming more and more unruly? We have! Neither of us can stand to go into a place of business and have to put up with racket made by some child whose parent has not bothered to teach them how to behave in public. Ever since they started passing laws that made it illegal to spank our children, they have gotten out of control. We say bust that child's butt! It is your responsibility to teach your children how to behave. It is not the school's place, or daycare's department, it is yours. If you can't control them, don't have them! If you already have them, then maybe someone should take them away. We are raising a generation of miscreant children, because "spanking your child is child abuse". Our Bibles say "Spare the rod, spoil the child." Guess the liberals missed that…

To make the problem worse, all of the sudden, the state wants to put our children on methamphetamine derived medications to treat the symptoms of "ADHD." Twenty years ago, there was no such thing as ADHD. That is nothing but the state's excuse for the fact that, since disciplining our children became illegal; they don't know how to act. If a teacher says that your child needs to be tested for ADHD and you refuse, or refuse to medicate your child, DHS gets involved.

What were we thinking when we allowed the government to control how we discipline our children? Yeah, we get the argument that there were some people who go too far and abuse their children, but most of us actually love our children, and are more responsible than that. As for those who are not, we have a legal system to take care of them. The problem is that parents get so frustrated by children who are out of control, that they themselves lose control. If we were allowed to discipline our children, then in most cases, it would never get to that point. See, humans truly do have a pack mentality. If our children don't learn from an early age who is the alpha male and female, they challenge that hierarchy at every opportunity.

But since spanking our children *on the behind with an open hand,* has somehow become akin to molesting them, our kids no longer know the difference between right and wrong. In fact, they don't even know that their actions have consequences. For instance, a recent study of high school students shows that only one out of every three knows the correlation between cause and effect.

Lack of punishment in the home/school system encourages children in a negative way. Our children no longer have to worry about being punished for unruly behavior, but we have a cure for that! It all started because of CJ. You see, she has a very odd rule of thumb, upon meeting other people's kids, she automatically dislikes them until it is proven to her that the child is well mannered, respectful, and well behaved. Why? You may ask. Simple. It is illegal to spank either the parents or the unruly child.

We say that the government should set the fine for beating the parents of unruly children at one dollar. We bet more people would control their children if they had to worry about being beaten themselves. It sounds funny, but we are only half joking. If parents were held responsible for the things they allow their children to get away with doing, those children would get away with a lot less.

Also, places of business should be able to post signs stating that they reserve the right to refuse service to the parents of unruly children. You know the signs that say, "No shoes, no shirt, no service"? Yeah, something like that. Bet that would help curb the problem, too. In addition, those of us who control our children would be able to do our shopping, etc. in peace.

Press one for English

Why is it that when I press one for English, I still can't
understand the person on the other end of the line? For
that matter, why do we have to press one at all? For
centuries, immigrants to our country have accepted the
fact that they should learn to speak English so that they
could become functional, productive members of our
society. In fact, before a person can take the citizenship
test, they are required to prove they are proficient in the
English language. If they cannot do so, they are required
to take English classes. What makes Hispanics any
different? What is so special about them that we have to
give up a portion of our identity in order to include
them? Oh yeah, it's not legal immigrants that we make
these exceptions for. You know, the ones who follow
those pesky immigration laws that we have in place. In
fact, if we were Hispanic, and had gone through the
whole naturalization process, we'd be insulted! What
gives these people the right to make a mockery of us by
circumventing our laws? Whatever happened to "When
in Rome…?" We can't think of any other country
wherein the natives to that country are being forced to
learn the languages of the country's immigrants. Last
time we checked, this was the United States of America,
and English was the language of our forefathers.

In every aspect of our lives, we have to choose between
English and Spanish. Why is that? Furthermore, we hate
the fact that in some states, it is mandatory for our
children to learn Spanish that they can interact with the
Spanish speaking children at school. What is that about?
For example, in some areas of California, children
cannot start kindergarten unless they can speak Spanish.

This is an outrage! It is absolutely preposterous. If they want to live here, *they* should learn *our* language, NOT the other way around.

Don't get us wrong, we have no problem with legal immigrants who come into this country, apply for citizenship or work visas, and do not try to take advantage of our systems. They move here, get jobs, and become productive members of society. That is perfectly alright. Milking our system is not. In fact, this is a slap in the face to those who are struggling to get their citizenship the legal way; those who study for months and months to learn our history and culture, and be able to pass the citizenship test. Furthermore, why is it that immigrants don't have to pay taxes but are eligible for tax based government welfare programs? If they want to be here, they should have to live by the same laws and limitations as those of us who are native to this country. That includes our welfare system. That system is burdened enough by lazy, oxygen theiving Americans; we shouldn't be adding illegal immigrants to the problem. If you don't see that they are a problem, take a good long look at California. Just the other day, a state government representative released a statement stating that they were no longer going to pay out welfare benefits or any of the like for illegal immigrants. The only thing illegal immigrants in California will now be eligible for is emergency health care. This also means no more prenatal care for those who see fit to jump the border at 8 months into their pregnancies and spit out a baby just so they can circumvent the entire immigration process for citizenship.

America, we have got to stand up! Our country can barely handle the burden of taking care of its legal citizens. Trying to take care of the illegal ones will cripple us. And it's not that we don't have laws in place to rectify the situation, we just don't enforce these laws. It is time to make our government work for us, rather than against us. It is time that we get the attention of our nation's leaders and let them know how we feel. Otherwise, we will one day wake up in an America that we no longer recognize. Please, we have to do something, if not for our own sakes, then for the sakes of our children.

Patriotically,

NLC & CJE

Immorality

Are we alone in wondering why it is that, less than a century ago, our children were well mannered, respectful, and had morals; yet today, they are the exact opposite? Let's take a moment to ponder all that has happened over the course of the last century. What's the big thing that comes to mind? For me, it's Women's Lib. Ladies, I know that I will offend quite a few of you by saying this, but Women's Lib is the worst thing that has ever happened to this country, indeed, the world.

When women started working outside of the home, and spending more and more time away from their children, this country started going downhill. Television and video games became our babysitters, and daycare centers began teaching our children socialism. I remember when most mothers stayed at home with their children, and we knew that education began at home. We did not leave it to the public school system to teach our children what was right and wrong; when Sunday morning values was something that every child was taught.

There was a time when young men were taught to be men; to grow up and be responsible, productive members of society. Now they are taught to look out for themselves and to succeed at any cost, regardless of who they have to step on to get there. Those that don't learn that lesson learn an equally destructive one: the world owes you everything, and its' okay to let others take care of you. Where are the men in this country??? What happened to a strong work ethic, and taking care of your family? Welfare was NOT designed to allow you to be lazy!!! It is supposed to be a hand up, not a hand out.

Ladies, don't think I forgot about you. Who gave you the right to leave your children's upbringing to the whims of the media and the government? Have any of you actually sat down and watched some of the television programs and video games that you allow to babysit your children? Do you know what they are learning from these shows and games? Unlawfulness, disrespect, and violence are the lessons they are taught, in addition to lying, stealing, cheating, and sexual immorality! For instance, a show that many of us grew up watching and loving is now teaching our children that homosexuality is okay. Why do Burt and Ernie have to be a married gay couple? For years, they were merely roommates, and that was okay. Why change it now???

Our children, our futures are coming home pierced, tattooed, and pregnant. Our daughters are putting "tramp stamps" on their backs, and they think that it is okay, they're just "expressing themselves". No wonder teenage pregnancy is such a rampant problem in this country. And don't get me started on abortion! There was a time that if a young girl was foolish enough to go out and have sex, she had to live with the consequences of her actions. Now, it is perfectly acceptable in our society for that same young girl to murder her unborn child. All that teaches our kids is that there are no consequences. They are free to do whatever they want to do, and we can just erase their mistakes. Where is our morality? Why are we as parents not taking the responsibility to teach our children what is right???

People say that we are progressing. What are we progressing toward?

Take me back to a time when people stood up for what they believed; not because it was popular, but because it was right. I want to go back to a time when people were not afraid to voice their opinions just because those opinions were unpopular. Ladies and gentlemen, I know that I am not the only person in this country who thinks this way. It is time for us to stand up! Stop being as sheep going meekly to the slaughter!! You have a voice, let it be heard!!!

If this post angers people, or causes me to ostracized, GOOD! I'm not trying to make people happy; I'm trying to make people think.

NLC

Pedophiles and their Liberal Buddies

Hey America,

It's time to talk about a rather delicate issue. Pedophilia. Why? Because I am sick to death of freaking bleeding heart liberals making excuses for the monsters that prey on our children. What brought this on? Why, Michael Jackson, of course. All of these people talking about what a hard life he had, blah, blah, blah. But lest we get accused of hating MJ, I'll say it's all pedophiles.

I get so sick of hearing these monsters tell us all how they were abused as kids, and it's all they know. They didn't realize that it was wrong. Whatever! I endured sixteen years of physical, sexual, and verbal abuse, and I didn't turn into a baby raper of a child abuser. Yes, I get that abuse is a cycle, and children learn what they live with. I know all the clichés. However, I also know that we as human beings have the strength to overcome our pasts, and that ultimately, we are responsible for who we become.

There are no excuses for preying on innocents. There is nothing that could happen to anyone that would ever make that okay, and as soon as we start making excuses for them, that's what we're doing. We are saying that it's okay to destroy the life of an innocent child, because after all, someone has to atone for the horrors that you lived through. Here's a novel idea! How about we hold the pedophiles and child abusers responsible for their actions??? How about, instead of giving them a slap on the wrist and maybe a couple of years in jail, we actually punish them. My idea is, for the first offense; make it an automatic minimum ten year sentence. That's not too harsh, considering that it will probably take the child ten years of therapy to get passed what happened. For a repeat offense, give them a life sentence or a lethal injection. Why? Because rape and pedophilia have the highest recidivism rates of any crime on the books. If they do it once, chances are, they will do it again. As for chemical castration, that doesn't work! They just switch to using instruments to represent the phallus. The end result is the same.

We need to hold them responsible for their crimes, and make them pay the consequences. There is no reason in the world that we should have to worry if our children are safe when they play outside. If these people actually had to worry about being punished for their crimes, I can guarantee, there would be less of these crimes to worry about! All I'm saying is that there should be a level of accountability in all aspects of our government. That accountability standard should be the same for everyone from the average citizen to the politicians. There should be no bleeding heart organizations that jump in to save the poor criminals from facing the consequences of their actions. If they can't do the time, they shouldn't do the crime. Period. End of discussion.

Chapter 8

Health Care and Other Atrocities

"My reading of history convinces me that most bad government results from too much government." Thomas Jefferson

Goodbye Private Insurance

Dear America,

As we write this letter, we're listening to talk radio:
Beck, Limbaugh, Hannity, and Boortz. In the news today
is another example of the movement to destroy
capitalism. In the healthcare bill that was recently
presented, effective on the day that this bill becomes
law, it will be illegal to buy and sell private insurance. If
you currently have insurance through your employer,
you can keep it, provided that (a) you don't leave your
job for any reason (b) your employer is able, financially,
to continue to provide insurance (c) your employer does
not elect to do away with employer provided healthcare.
Given the wording of this bill, I am left to assume that
COBRA will be a thing of the past. We will no longer
have the option to maintain our healthcare coverage
upon termination of employment.

As if Medicare and Medicaid weren't bad enough, now
we're facing government run healthcare for everyone.
But that isn't even the worst of it! Our taxes are going to
be raised to astronomical levels to pay for this program.
According to the New York Post, tax rates in that state,
for those families earning $150,000 or more a year will
see their taxes rates raised to between 53 and 56%. I'm
not just talking about single people; I mean couples
whose combined gross income reaches this level. Now,
consider the cost of living in that state. People pay over
$1000 a month for slum apartments there. $100,000 a
year is nothing! Its middle class! What happened to no

tax increases for people making less than $200,000 a year?

Imagine going to college, working hard to get a good education, then finally graduating, going out and, if you're lucky, finding a job. You feel proud, as if you've really accomplished something. You think all your work has paid off. Your new employer tells you that you will be earning the equivalent of $35 per hour, and you think that you will be able, with a little saving, to do all of the things that you always wanted to do. Then you get your first paycheck and discover that, for all of your preparation and hard work, you are only earning, after taxes, $18.55 per hour. You realize that you could have earned the same amount if, instead of going to school, you had gone to work in a factory. How does that knowledge make you feel? We hope that you are as outraged as we are. In this country, where we are encouraged to go to school, get an education, and work hard for our futures, the rewards of that hard work are being stripped from us. What happened to "the pursuit of happiness"? By the way, for those of you from a younger generation who were educated in the public school system, that is a fundamental part of the first amendment, derived from the Social Contract.

Still think the government has our best interests at heart? If so, you are oblivious. Wake up! Open your eyes, pay attention, and stand up for what is left of the country we grew up knowing and loving!!! This is the country for which our fathers and grandfathers bled and died. On the up side, there is a new poll out that shows that 78% of Americans no longer support Obamacare. Thank GOD! There is hope for us yet. We know there is. We know that we are not alone in this. We know that we can't be the only person who wants to stop this onslaught against liberty. America, please, we have got to do something!

As I cook dinner for my family, I am struggling to breathe around the very large lump in my throat. I think of the America that I used to know and love, and compare that to the America that we are headed toward. I think of all the freedoms that we have enjoyed and taken for granted. I cannot staunch the flow of tears as I realize, once again, that the America that I know will seem like a fairy tale to my children, unless we do something, and do it now. We no longer have the option of procrastinating, or waiting to see what will happen next. If we don't act soon, we will lose the opportunity, and the freedom to do so.

Ladies and gentlemen, it is time now to make our stand. Hannity has posted the email addresses of all of the nation's congressmen on his web page. These addresses will be available within twenty-four hours. Email your congressmen, organize rallies, raise nine kinds, and let them know that we will not stand by while they crush our economy beyond repair. Let them know that if they pass this bill, that they will NOT win a re-election. Don't let them do this to us. The Federal Reserve is already predicting that we will not see any new jobs created for the next five to six years. That means that unemployment is not going to decrease, in fact it will go up; especially if this bill is passed. The added tax burden alone will force small businesses to either decrease jobs, or close their doors. There will be NO growth. This will be the straw that breaks the camel's back, we guarantee it.

America's Deadly Secret

The early twentieth century saw the birth and initial rise of the progressive movement. These are the people that Senator Hillary Clinton has called "great Americans." Among the causes championed by these progressives was the idea that Sir Francis Galton called eugenics. While the word itself may seem innocuous, the idea is anything but. For those of you who do not know, here is the definition according to the Columbia Encyclopedia:

> Eugenics - the study of, or belief in, the possibility of improving the qualities of the human species or a human population by such means as discouraging reproduction by persons having genetic defects or presumed to have inheritable undesirable traits (negative eugenics) or encouraging reproduction by persons presumed to have inheritable desirable traits (positive eugenics)."[2] Prominent in the late 19th century and the Progressive Era, eugenics became a core tenet of some of the policies behind Adolf Hitler's Nazi regime.

American scientist Charles Davenport is responsible for eugenics' transformation from a scientific idea to a worldwide movement that was later implemented by many countries, the US included. In 1904, he established the Biological Experiment Station at Cold Spring Harbor, and the Eugenics Records Office in 1910. These offices were responsible for the scientific basis that was later enacted as government policy. In 1925, he became the first President of the International Federation of Eugenics Organizations. Other prominent US eugenicists include

Harry Laughlin, Irving Fischer, Madison Grant and Lucien Howe.

During the twentieth century, a number of studies were conducted that seemed to prove that certain mental illnesses such as bipolar disorder, schizophrenia, and depression were hereditary. Eugenicists immediately pounced on these findings as proof for their cause. In the late 1800s and early 1900s, states laws were implemented that prohibited marriage and forced the sterilization of those with mental illness, with the intent of preventing those people from passing on their defective genes. In 1927, the US Supreme Court upheld those laws, and they were not abolished until the mid twentieth century. Approximately 64,000 Americans were sterilized between 1907 and 1963. California led the pack, and performed most sterilization procedures with little or no due process. In the first twenty-five years of eugenic legislation, California sterilized 9,782 people, most of whom were women. Many of these were classified as "bad girls," with such diagnoses as "passionate," "oversexed" or "sexually wayward." At Sonoma, some women were even sterilized because of what was deemed an abnormally large clitoris or labia. What?!!!

In 1933, some 1,278 coercive sterilizations were performed. Of that number, 700 were performed on women. The state's two leading sterilization facilities for that year were Sonoma State Home with 388 operations and Patton State Hospital with 363 operations. Other sterilization centers included Agnews, Mendocino, Napa, Norwalk, Stockton and Pacific Colony state hospitals.

As we mentioned earlier, even the US Supreme Court advocated eugenics. In the 1927 decision in the Buck v Bell case, Supreme Court Justice Oliver Wendell Holmes wrote, "It is better for all the world, if instead of waiting to execute degenerate offspring for crime, or to let them starve for their imbecility, society can prevent those who are manifestly unfit from continuing their kind.... Three generations of imbeciles are enough." That is a shockingly sickening statement, especially coming from a man who was a Supreme Court justice. What is not surprising about this statement is that during the Nuremburg trials, many Nazis quoted it as part of their defense. They also used the fact that eugenics was a widely accepted concept, especially in the United States.

The executive secretary of the American Eugenics Society, Leon Whitney declared, "While we were pussy-footing around...the Germans were calling a spade a spade." In a 1934 *Richmond Times-Dispatch* article, Joseph DeJarnette, superintendent of Virginia's Western State Hospital stated "The Germans are beating us at our own game." These people held the Germans in high esteem, counted them as heroes to the cause. How sickening is that? There are many other quotes, but we think that what we have provided will suffice. One other interesting little tidbit of information, the Planned Parenthood movement, founded by Margaret Sanger, was, and is simply another application of eugenics. Its purpose is to provide contraceptives, and even abortion, to those of lower classes, who are deemed unfit or undesirable. If you have any doubts about this, Google her.

However, that's all just lead in information to the main point of this letter. We have talked at length about the Obamacare issue, and we have discussed the fact that this bill has clauses in it that will basically ration healthcare, with preference going to those between the ages 15 and 40. The reason being that people in that age range have received maximum investments from society, and are still of an age to be productive members of society. Those younger than age 15 have not had as much time and money invested in them, and would therefore not waste the state's efforts if they are not allowed to live. Conversely, those over the age of 40 have begun to decline in health. They are nearing the age of retirement, and being eligible for Medicare and social security. Therefore, it is expedient for the state to allow them to pass on, before they cost the state anymore money. In fact, Obama's Healthcare Czar, Ezekiel Emanuel gives credence to this with his many statements, and his "Complete Lives System."

Here are a few quotes from Dr. Emanuel himself to illustrate this. "Vague promises of savings from cutting waste, enhancing prevention and wellness, installing electronic medical records and improving quality are merely 'lipstick' cost control, more for show and public relations than for true change," (Health Affairs Feb. 27, 2008). "Doctors take the Hippocratic Oath too seriously, as an imperative to do everything for the patient regardless of the cost or effects on others" (Journal of the American Medical Association, June 18, 2008). He says medical care should be reserved for the non-disabled, not given to those "who are irreversibly prevented from being or becoming participating citizens . . . An obvious example is not guaranteeing health services to patients with dementia" (Hastings Center Report, Nov.-Dec. '96). "Unlike allocation by sex or race, allocation by age is not invidious discrimination; every person lives through different life stages rather than being a single age. Even if 25-year-olds receive priority over 65-year-olds, everyone who is 65 years now was previously 25 years" (Lancet, Jan. 31). That ought to be enough to tell you what this guy is really about.

We have all heard proponents of the healthcare tell us that rationing will never happen, that such statements are just another ruse used by anti-Obama and anti-healthcare rightwing extremists. However, what they neglect to admit is the fact that merely instituting this bill will add to the economic crisis that we are already experiencing. The lack of funds will necessitate rationing. We won't be able to provide healthcare to everyone at the same levels that we currently do. They expect us to believe, in spite of all evidence to the contrary, that the same system that Great Britain and Canada have will work here with no adverse effects. We wonder how that's going to work.

Unfortunately, this is not the only pro-eugenics portion of this piece of legislation. Please read the following in its entirety, and then go to the bill and read it in context.

SEC. 431. DISCLOSURES TO CARRY OUT HEALTH INSURANCE EXCHANGE SUBSIDIES.

 (a) IN GENERAL.—Subsection (l) of section 6103 of the Internal Revenue Code of 1986 is amended by adding at the end the following new paragraph: ''(21) DISCLOSURE OF RETURN INFORMATION TO CARRY OUT HEALTH INSURANCE EXCHANGE SUBSIDIES.—

''(A) IN GENERAL.—The Secretary, upon written request from the Health Choices Commissioner or the head of a State-based health insurance exchange approved for operation under section 208 of the America's Affordable

Health Choices Act of 2009, shall disclose to officers and employees of the Health Choices Administration or such State-based health insurance exchange, as the case may be, return information of any taxpayer whose income is relevant in determining any affordability credit described in subtitle C of title II of the America's Affordable Health Choices Act of 2009. Such return information shall be limited to—

''(i) taxpayer identity information with respect to such taxpayer,

 ''(ii) the filing status of such taxpayer,

''(iii) the modified adjusted gross income of such taxpayer (as defined in section 59B(e)(5)),

''(iv) the number of dependents of the taxpayer,

''(v) such other information as is prescribed by the Secretary by regulation as

might indicate whether the taxpayer is eligible for such affordability credits (and the amount thereof), and

''(vi) the taxable year with respect to which the preceding information relates or, if applicable, the fact that such information is not available.

''(B) RESTRICTION ON USE OF DISCLOSED INFORMATION.—Return information disclosed under subparagraph (A) may be used by officers and employees of the Health Choices Administration or such State-based health insurance exchange, as the case may be, only for the purposes of, and to the extent necessary in, establishing and verifying the appropriate amount of any affordability credit described in subtitle C of title II of the America's Affordable Health Choices Act of 2009 and providing for the repayment of any such credit which was in excess of such appropriate amount.''

We believe that, in addition to healthcare rationing by age, it will also be rationed based on socioeconomic status. There is no other reason for the Health Care Commissioner to need your tax files. The bill says so that "they may establish and verify the appropriate amount of any affordability credit." If you believe that, then you belong firmly in the category of people who actually trust these people. We don't, not for a second.

For that reason, we ask that you continue to stand, even in the face of fierce opposition. Do not let your guard down, and do not allow the progressives to silence you.

No matter how many times they call you "right wing extremist" or "Astroturf" or any other of the myriad of names that they have chosen for us, stand up. No matter how many of their thugs attack us, stand up, and when they try to destroy you, and try to frighten us into acquiescence, stand up. They can only knock down so many of us. We outnumber them. We are 60% of the country's population; that makes them the minority.

"Facts are stubborn things; and whatever may be our wishes, our inclinations, or the dictates of our passions, they cannot alter the state of facts and evidence." John Adams.

Chips, Anyone?

America,

Have you ever had the feeling that you were speeding along on a roller coaster, and the brakes were out, so there was no way to stop? That's how we feel right now. For weeks, we have been writing these letters, venting our feelings in what we hoped would be a constructive way. It has helped, in that we no longer feel completely overwhelmed by all of this mess. We are finally able to hold our heads above water and breathe before the next onslaught. We hope you're ready, America, 'cause here it comes. The next wave of assaults are even more destructive than the previous ones.

Over the past couple of days, we have been studying several legislative bills that are either currently up for vote, or have recently been passed. We gotta tell ya, we are beyond disturbed. The first bill is one that we are sure you are somewhat familiar with. It's the new healthcare bill; HR 3200. Now, most American people know by now that this thing is a monstrosity. What you may not know is that there is actually language in that bill that suggests things that are tantamount to assisted suicide. For seniors and people who suffer from serious disabilities, and/or dementia, there will be mandated counseling sessions to discuss different suicide methods. (Wait a minute, isn't suicide illegal? What are they gonna do, put you in jail, or a mental ward somewhere, if you fail?) This is sickening! We don't understand how this country got to the point that state assisted suicide is even a possibility. What is going on? And is it just us who feel that this is just wrong, on every level?

Two other atrocities just recently passed the House Appropriations Committee. If you value freedom and privacy, these will infuriate you. One is the appropriated budget for the Department of Homeland Security (HR 2892). You've got to love that word: *appropriated.* For once, the government tells the truth. Anyway, in this budget, on page 27, is the following sentence:

That not less than $28,000,000 of unobligated balances of prior year appropriations shall remain available and be obligated solely for implementation of a biometric air exit capability.

Wait a second, *biometric?* You mean like microchips? Really? This section is concerning immigration, so some of you may think that biometric tracking of immigrants may be a good thing. Let's move on to the next piece of legislation, shall we?

This lovely piece of art has been named HR 2028, the New Employee Verification Act of 2009. Sounds innocuous enough, doesn't it? Maybe even something you can get behind. Not so much. Allow us to tell you why. If you do a little digging into this bill, Page 40 to be exact, you will find the following treasure:

1 "(A) IDENTITY AUTHENTICATION AND EMPLOYMENT ELIGIBILITY VERIFICATION BY EN

ROLLMENT PROVIDERS.—the SEEVS (Secure Employment Eligibility Verification System) shall utilize the services of private sector entities (herein after in this subsection referred to as 'enrollment providers'), with appropriate expertise, which shall be subject to initial and periodic certification by the Commissioner, to provide—

"(i) enrollment under the SEEVS of new employees by means of identity authentication in a manner that provides a high level of certainty as to their true identities, using immigration and identifying information maintained by the Social Security Administration and the Department of Homeland Security, review of identity documents, and background screening verification techniques using publicly available information;

"(ii) protection of the authenticated information through <u>biometric</u> technology; and

"(iii) verification of employment eligibility of such new employees.

There's that word again. Funny how it keeps popping up, isn't it. Once again it's used to pertain to immigrants. I guess they think that we are more likely to accept it if they are using it on someone else. However, we ask you to bear in mind that, if they will do this to citizens of other countries, they will do it to US citizens too. The point is to start with steps that the American people will either support or, at the very least, grudgingly accept. Once they lay the infrastructure for this type of thing, it will no longer matter if we will accept it or not. All they need is to get their foot in the door.

It is obvious that we have either elected far too many "progressives", or far too few people who are conscientious enough to actually read the legislation before casting their votes. Our guess is that it is, sadly, a combination of the two. On the one hand, we have a group of left wing radicals who want to transform our country under the guise of making it better, and on the other, we have the "old guard" who, quite frankly, have been in Washington far too long, and need to be put out to pasture. With a combination like this, America is doomed. James Madison had it exactly right: "It will be of little avail to the people that the laws are made by men of their own choice if the laws be so voluminous that they cannot be read, or so incoherent that they cannot be understood."

We are only two women, living our lives, and digging up what we can when we can. If we found these three bills so easily, imagine how many others are floating around out there. Ladies and gentlemen, the time for burying our heads in the sand has passed. We can no longer turn a blind eye to what these liberal politicians are doing behind our backs. We have to ferret out this information, and pass it along to anyone who will listen. There is no other way to stop these people. If you love this country, do your part to make sure that it doesn't get transformed into something we no longer recognize.

P.S. Just for fun, go to www.govtrack.us. Type in the word biometrics, and see how many bills pop up. In fact, you can research any bill there. We warn you though, you may be amazed at what you find.

HUH???

You know, sometimes being right is NOT a good thing. This is one of those times. Recently, several talk radio hosts have quoted some of the House Democrats in saying that they will pass the healthcare bill without the help of the Republicans. Even worse, President Obama said that he would pass it with or without the votes in Congress. Huh? Can he even do that? Unfortunately, the answer is yes, he can. For one, all he needs is sixty votes to pass it in congress. For two, if he can't get those votes, he can and will use reconciliation. Reconciliation is the budget approval process, and requires only fifty one votes to pass. In other words, the liberals can basically back door this bill into law. Isn't that wonderful?

You know, everyone has talked a lot about the financial cost of enacting this monstrosity, but very few people have discussed the other costs. Like the loss of personal freedoms in choosing a healthcare plan, the fact that, if this bill is passed, then there will be no private healthcare in ten or fifteen years. It will be illegal. But that's not even the worst of it. There are clauses in this bill that would make our founding fathers turn in their graves so violently that it could cause an earthquake along the entire eastern seaboard. (We're only half joking.)

Allow us to tell you some of the specifics. Let's start with healthcare rationing. On page 29, there are limits placed on how much the government will pay per person and per family. For those of you who don't know what that means, you will only be allowed a certain number of doctor visits. If you have a chronic ailment, you will not be able to be able to get anywhere near the same level of care as you can now. In fact, there will be a Health Benefits Advisory Committee, and a Health Choices Commissioner to decides what treatments will be available and to whom. What right has anyone else to decide what kind of care you get besides you and your doctor?

Then there's this one: page 50, section 152, states that this bill will provide coverage to everyone in this country; citizen and non-citizen, legal and illegal alike. Doesn't it make you feel good to know that your tax dollars will go to pay for healthcare for illegal aliens and non citizens? How is it right that people who do not pay taxes in this country are entitled to healthcare benefits paid for by our taxes? We wish this was the worst thing in this bill, but unfortunately, it's not.

Next on the list of atrocities is the implementation of a national medical ID card, (On page 58) and trust us, it won't stop at a card. They will use this as another excuse to push for microchips. We guarantee it. We say this because on page 59, there is a provision allowing the government access to our bank accounts to "allow automated reconciliation" of services. We don't trust these people to have access to any of our personal information. If we had our way, they wouldn't even know our birthdays.

For those of you who wasted your time and went to medical school, you'll no longer be making the money you thought you would. Page 127 gives the government the right to decide how much money you will make. Aren't you just thrilled with that prospect? Ironically, we both considered going into the mental health field at one point in time. Boy, are we glad we decided not to do that! Now you can all look forward to some neo-con deciding that you make too much money, and therefore deciding to take a large portion of it away. Lucky you!

Now, we have only covered the contents of the first 130 pages. Do you really think it doesn't get worse the further into the bill that you get? Allow us to disabuse you of that nonsensical notion. This 1018 page equivalent of a communist manifesto is packed full of sections and provisions that give these jackals more and more power while stripping of us of our freedoms and liberties. If you haven't yet read this bill, and don't know what's in it, go to www.govtrack.us and download the pdf file. The only way that we can stop these people is by being informed. If you still think these people have your best interests in mind, wake up! Please step away from the Ambien...

Chapter 9

Crazy Train: the Unpopular Opinion

"The strongest reason for the people to retain the right to keep and bear arms is, as a last resort, to protect themselves against tyranny in government." Thomas Jefferson

Conspiracy Theory

Ladies and gentlemen, fellow Americans, have you ever
wished that you could turn back time, and unlearn
something? Or wished that you make a thing untrue,
simply by pretending it doesn't exist? I feel that way
right now, much to my chagrin. You see, I have an
insatiable thirst for knowledge, a need to know
everything that's going on in the world. I don't know
why, I just do. Sometimes that thirst for knowledge puts
me in an untenable position. I dig up information that I
wish I didn't. This is certainly one of those times. This
particular subject is controversial, to say the least, and
not one of my favorites. The problem is that, once I dig
up this kind of information, I have to share it. My
conscience won't let me do otherwise. So, I am going to
go out on a major limb. I realize that many of you who
read this letter will write me off as a conspiracy theorist,
or a right wing nut. I realize that there are those of you
who will read very little of this. That being said, here
goes.

Most, if not all, of you have heard the stories, innuendos,
and the paranoid rumors, that the power elite in this
country are trying to form an American Union, styled
after the European Union. You've heard the talking
heads who have told you that it's just a myth. The
politicians deny even the possibility of it. Yet, much to
my surprise, it's true. Not that it will be what the Alex
Jones' of the world say it will be. But I'm not saying it
won't be either. Here is what I have learned:

> On March 13, 2005, US Commerce Secretary,
> Carlos M. Gutierrez met with Mexican Secretary

of Economy, Fernando Canales and Canadian Privy Council Assistant Secretary Phil Ventura. Ten days after this meeting, at a trilateral summit held in Waco, TX, the leaders of those three countries announced the formation of the Security and Prosperity Partnership of North America (SPP). It was described as "the roadmap to opportunity and overcoming challenges presented by an ever changing world" by Canadian Prime Minister Paul Martin. The problem is, this was not even brought to our congress for a vote. In fact, most members of congress do not even know that the SPP exists. What's worse is that the "working groups" put in place to by this partnership make serious recommendations at the cabinet level of all three governments.

Howard Phillips, who is a major critic of the SPP, believes that this act is identical to the beginnings of the European Union.

90 days after its formation, the SPP released the first of its Report to Leaders. It's recommendation? Form more working groups, one of which was called The North American Competitiveness Council (NACC). The purpose of the NACC is to get private sector business executives to push their agenda. Free trade among the countries is always desirable, and who better to push for it than those who have the money to pay the lobbyists? The purpose of this group is to take the integration of the continent beyond the North American Free Trade

Agreement (NAFTA). In the February 2007 Report to Leaders, one of the suggestions to the government heads was that they "Consider the use of enhanced technology and infrastructure including RFID and biometric identifiers in combination with special processing lanes at border points." Further stating that "A single, interoperable credential should be used for all programs directed at identified low-risk people so that they can cross the border with minimal or no interference. (And we wonder why no one has done anything about border security...) Not surprisingly, the very existence of this organization is kept pretty quiet. In fact, the people involved in this project are so concerned with the secrecy of it, that they have contracted private consultants to create blueprints, roadmaps, etc. in order to circumvent the freedom of information act. Makes me wonder how they can be surprised that people don't trust the government. I mean, they *say* that they are not a threat to any nation's sovereignty, but if you buy that, I've got some oceanfront property in Arizona that I would *love* to talk to you about.

Enter everyone's favorite secret organization, the Council on Foreign Relations (CFR). Founded in 1921, the CFR a "non-partisan and independent membership organization" that is "dedicated to the belief that the nation's peace and prosperity is firmly linked to that of the rest of the world." I'll buy that, but with the caveat that it is not as innocuous as it sounds. Caroll Quigley, late Georgetown history professor, Bill Clinton

mentor, and CFR supporter said of the CFR "the Council on Foreign Relations is the American branch of a society which originated in England and believes that national boundaries should be obliterated, and one world rule established."
In 2005, the CFR released a seventy page report called "Building a North American Community". The findings were then presented to congress. Yes, our congress. The report is important because it contains "specific advice on how the SPP can be pursued and realized." The most important suggestion is this: "the task force proposes the creation, by 2010, of a North American Community to enhance security, prosperity, and opportunity. Its boundaries will be defined by a common external tariff and an outer security perimeter within which the movement of people, products, and capital will be legal, orderly, and safe. Its goal will be to guarantee a free, secure, just and prosperous North America." The report also recommended the creation of a North American Advisory Council that "should be composed of eminent persons from outside the government to provide a public voice for North America along the lines of the Bilderberg Conferences."
CFR supporter, Robert Pastor suggests that a North American Investment Fund be created to spend 20 billion dollars per year for ten years on infrastructure to connect Southern Mexico with the rest of North America. He follows that by stating that the Department of Homeland Security should expand to provide "Continental Security." Develop new North American highways and high

speed rail corridors to facilitate freer movement within the continent. He goes on to say "Instead of stopping North Americans at the borders, we should provide them with a secure *biometric* border pass that would ease transit across the border, kind of like an easy pass permits our cars to speed through those toll booths." Uh, excuse me??? As if that weren't enough, he keeps talking, saying that "the US and Canada should begin to merge immigration and refugee policies." (Personally, I wish someone would shut this guy up!) Unfortunately, no one does.

Next on the acronym line up we have the North American Forum (NAF). NAF is an incredibly secretive group of "extremely high level elites". Additionally, it is a sister organization, and parallel structure of the SPP. It is another of those organizations that keeps absolutely no public records. (Don't you love those?) In 2006, they had a conference at the Banff Springs Hotel in Alberta, Canada. Although there were no announcements made to the public, and no reporters on scene, we know about this conference. How do we know? One of the guests was so outraged at the discussions held during the conference that she spoke out. She said that the topics covered were an affront to democracy. And this is one of the attendees. I can just imagine what the rest of us would think if we were privy to those conversations.

Now, all of that having been said, I invite you to research these findings for yourself. Don't depend on what I say here to be your sole source of information. As I have reiterated time and again, the purpose of these letters is to inspire you to think. Also, I do hope to shake you out of your comfort zone, and get you to open your eyes to the world around you.

"When men yield up the privilege of thinking, the last shadow of liberty quits the horizon." Thomas Paine.

Politically Incorrect

Well, it's finally time to talk about what everyone is talking about NOT talking about. Yep, you guessed it, race. (With a few related topics thrown in for good measure.)

Over the last few years, everything has become so "politically correct". In fact, it's gotten so ridiculous that you can't say anything, good or bad, without being accused of being a racist. Now, most of us are mature enough to know that race-baiting, bigotry, and name calling signifies both a lack of maturity and intelligence. The issue of race is often used to incite feelings of sympathy and/or guilt, or to intimidate a specific target. We all learned this in grade school while dealing with the school yard bully.

It's rather reminiscent of a two year old who uses the plea of hunger when he or she gets called down for misbehaving. The child is smart enough to know that such a plea will not be ignored by a loving and responsible adult. In today's society, race baiting is being used in much the same way. Sadly, Americans are worse about this than any other society. What an accomplishment! We should be so proud. Seriously, GROW UP!!!!

Slavery ended a long time ago. Nobody owes you anything. You have the exact same opportunities in this country as everyone else. We mean, reparations may have been in order when slavery was abolished. Not so much now. For crying out loud, get over the ghetto "life's so hard, nobody wants to hand me everything on a silver platter" mentality. Get up off of your lazy behind, go find a job, actually show up and do your job, and the most amazing thing will happen! You'll be able to afford to buy the things that you need, for example, a car and a house. That doesn't mean to go get on welfare and get the state to pay your rent and buy your food, while you sell drugs or work under the table so you can buy a $40,000+ car and "pimp it out." That's not the American way; that's the lazy way.

What makes it worse is that it's not just race that we are so overly sensitive about. It's everything. It's about race, gender, religion, ethnicity, deviant sexual practices, violent proclivities, and even socio-economical standing. Give us a break! This is not America circa 1809. It's 2009. We have equal rights for everyone. Women and people of all ethnic backgrounds have the same rights as white men. However, not all the changes in equal rights have been good ones. For instance, criminals should not have more rights than their victims. If you commit homicide, your life should be forfeit. If you molest or otherwise abuse a child, you should not get a fine and or an 18 month prison sentence. You should get life. After all, that child will suffer the consequences of your actions for the rest of his or her life. If you grow up to be a serial killer, it's not your mom or dad's fault, it's yours. You make the choice to do what you do; you should have to pay the consequences. We'll even go a little further. If you decide that you want to live your life as a homosexual, you have to deal with everything that comes with that. You are choosing to live outside the laws of God, the very laws that this country was founded upon. As a result, you have to get used to the fact that people do not like what you do. Frankly, we are offended by it.

The point is, we all have equal rights. That should be enough. No one in this country should get special treatment based on the fact that they belong to a "minority group." When that is the status quo, we all pay the price. Nobody wins, least of all the American citizens.

P.S. Whatever happened to being a nation of proud Americans? Instead of playing the victim, as so many of us seem content to do, why can't we be proud of our respective heritages? Why can we not embrace the diversity of all of the cultures, and our respective histories? Instead of trying to whitewash history, and erase all the "bad" things that happened, we should embrace it and say, "look how far we've come." America is a melting pot of all races, cultures, and ethnicities. We should be proud of that, not ashamed.

Hardwired

Alright, America!

Are you ready to take another ride on the crazy train? All Aboard! Next stop, Conspiracy Road. Do you remember watching movies like, Conspiracy Theory with Mel Gibson, and Enemy of The State starring Will Smith? If you're anything like us, you probably thought that, while they were great movies, they were nothing more than the product of someone's overactive imagination. That's still true, but after the research that we did for this letter, we're beginning to wonder if someone in Hollywood somehow gained access to state secrets, and was trying to warn us through movies. Honestly, our rose colored glasses came off a long time ago, but we never, in a million years, would have imagined that things would ever get to this point. Not in this country, anyway.

Now that you are probably hopelessly lost trying to follow our ramblings, let us explain. We'll start by giving you the names of two companies that you *need* to check into: Digital Angel and Odin Technologies. Go ahead, Google them; follow the dead links, get frustrated, try another link, when that doesn't work, try another search engine. Repeat the process several times. When you finally hit the goldmine, don't say we didn't warn you. (In all fairness, we should tell you that this process could take an hour or so.) We'll start by telling you about the research process, then we'll tell you what we found. (And no skipping ahead!)

When we first started this search, we started in the most obvious, and we thought, easiest place. We started with Verichip Corporation. We clicked on three different links on this company's page, only to discover that all three links were dead. Hmmm. Okay, we'll try a different tack. A little digging led us to the fact that this company was once owned by Applied Digital Solutions. So, naturally, we tried to go to their web site. It's dead. At first we thought this was a mistake; we'd typed the address wrong or some such, so we tried again. Still no luck. How could a multibillion dollar *digital solutions* company not have a web site in this day and age? We know this company still exists, because it trades on the stock market.

Still, we are nothing if not stubborn, so these dead ends made us more determined than ever to dig up something. Next, we tried the Digital Angel web site, (by this time we're thinking to ourselves, "If this page is dead, we're going to scream!")And we *finally* started to make a progress. Still, there was not as much information as we thought there would be. For all that we had heard about these companies' ties to our government, there was a suspicious lack of information. We started to think that this would turn out to be a debunking letter. Still, we plodded on.

This time though, we got smart, instead of trying to follow the links on DA's web site, when we found something interesting, we googled it in another browser tab. This worked a whole lot better! Through this process, we found several caches of information. We told you, we're stubborn. We absolutely refused to give up, even when, several hours into our research, all we had were crumbs. In our minds, the crumbs had to lead to somewhere, and we're just tenacious enough to dig until we find out. Finally, all the pieces began to fall into place. Up to a certain point, there was a very definite, very direct link between the federal government and Verichip

Corporation. You didn't have to connect any dots to figure it out; it was all there, easy to find, not hidden at all. Then, suddenly, that link disappears. It's as if one side or the other suddenly decided to call the partnership quits. The catch was that there was no other indication that this was the case. The trail simply turned cold. That didn't make any sense to me. (I don't know about you, but we're just naturally inclined to be suspicious. That being the case, we had to keep digging.)

We kept going, and two hours later, we found the crumbs again! This time they were bigger than before, and we knew we were on the right track. After just a half hour, we hit pay dirt! We figured out not only why the trail had ended, but also why it was so hard to pick it back up. (As it turns out, it was so obvious that we didn't see it at first.) Now we will lay it out all nice and neat for you, and save you the headache that we went through. You're welcome.

Since Verichip is where we began our research, it is where we will begin the explanation. Here's what we found:

1. Verichip Corporation is a wholly owned subsidiary of Applied Digital Solutions.
2. Applied Digital Solutions is the beneficial owner of Digital Angel Corporation.

3. In March of 2003, ADS' Government Telecommunications (GTI), a subsidiary of Computer Equity, Inc, was awarded a multiyear contract from the federal government's General Services Administration.
4. In October 2004, Verichip Corporation won FDA approval for the first, and only, human implantable passive RFID microchip.
5. On July 18, 2005, Senators Michael Enzi (R-WY), and Senator Edward Kennedy (D-Mass) along with 36 other co-sponsors, introduced the "Wired for Healthcare Quality Act"
6. This bill passed the Senate with unanimous approval, and was referred to the Subcommittee on Health December 16, 2005.
7. That was the last action taken on this bill, and it died at the end of the session.
8. Trail dies until 2008.
9. 2008, Verichip comes up with Verimed's Health Link. Health Link is the use of a pRFID, in conjunction with an online database, which links your medical records to you.
10. April 2008 – Verichip sells its VeriTrace System (for disaster relief and emergency management needs) to two New Jersey counties.
11. November 2008 – Verichip announces that Health Link will be accessible through Microsoft Health Vault.
12. Wednesday, May 13, 2009 in **News:** RFID solutions provider ODIN Technologies has been awarded a comprehensive government-wide purchasing vehicle contract by the U.S. Federal Government's General Services Administration (GSA). The purchasing vehicle, or schedule,

authorizes government users to purchase RFID solutions and services which best suit their needs. (Article located on Odin' web page.)

13. Friday, July 10, 2009 in **News**: Precise Biometrics, a developer of biometric solutions, has been awarded a contract valued at more than $6.1 million from the U.S. government. The contract specifies Precise provides immediate delivery to various agencies with hardware and software necessary for the existing infrastructure involving Precise's Match-On-Card system.

14. ODIN is a prime contract holder for Passive RFID which is a United States Department of Defense (DoD) and NATO wide purchasing vehicle for passive RFID engineering and deployments services, hardware, software and solutions. PM J-AIT is the Joint Product Manager for Automatic Identification Technologies for the DoD.

Do we really need to list anything more? We've given you all of the pertinent information that we could find. If you are still curious, we're sorry but you're on your own. The gist of all of this is that our government has invested heavily in RFID technology; the most frightening aspect of which is the implantable RFID chips. As we illustrated in the biometrics letter, the lawmakers are trying very hard to find ways to implement all aspects of RFID's biometric technology. The problem is that there are so few people who know what's going on. This is compounded by the fact that many of the people who are aware have damaged their credibility by passing on false information. Most people now see them as crazy conspiracy theorists. That is a sad fact because, while they may be way off base in a lot of areas, they are dead

on in others. In order to preserve our credibility, we
invite you, in fact, we urge you, to research everything
we have said. Do *not* take our word for it, and do not
write us off as just another couple of loonies. We're not.
Believe us, this is one instance in which we wish we were
wrong.

Epilogue

Ladies and Gentlemen,

It is our humble hope and earnest wish that you have read this book in the spirit in which it was written. It is our intent to inform you, cause you to think, and, if possible, stir you into action. The America that we all grew up knowing and loving is beginning to dissappear. If things continue at their current rate, then our children and grandchildren will live in a twisted parody of the America that we had. America, we have to stand up! We have to stand now, before it's too late!

Please don't misunderstand us. It took a lot of prayer and soul searching for us to decide to put our feelings into words, especially words on paper. However, we felt like we no longer had a choice. Thomas Paine said, "He that would make his own liberty secure, must guard even his enemy from oppression; for if he violates this duty, he establishes a precedent that will reach to himself." That was part of what drove us to action, but only part. The most important reason, aside from of our children, is the fact that, as Christians, it is our duty to help our brothers and sisters, our neighbors. That is what we are trying to do. We are trying to help you by giving you some of the information that you need to possess, in order to be able to fight back and protect our country.

Please, as you read these last few words, reflect on the letters we've written here. Then, get on your knees, and ask God what He wants you to do. Ask him what your role in this is. Then stand up, pledge yourself to this cause, and do your part. Please.

"We must, indeed, all hang together or, most assuredly, we shall all hang separately."

Benjamin Franklin.

Special Thanks To:

GOD Almighty, without whom none of this would be possible. Our families, *Especially our Moms*! Siblings, Spouse, the Kiddos, close friends who encouraged us the whole way. You know who you are. Also, thank you, Glenn Beck, who has been a major inspiration to both of us. We love you guys! Most of all, thank you Mr. T. Lattimore, for encouraging us to think for ourselves, and starting the fire that has become a conflagration within us both.

Your Notes:

www.ingramcontent.com/pod-product-compliance
Lightning Source LLC
Chambersburg PA
CBHW020241290526
45784CB00003B/1068